COPING SUCCESSFULLY WITH MIGRAINE

SUE DYSON was brought up on Merseyside, and qualified as a translator before becoming a secretary. A graduate in French and English, she passed the Private and Executive Secretary's Diploma exams with the highest marks ever awarded. She is now a full-time writer and translator, though she 'keeps her hand in' with occasional temping and teaching. Her books for Sheldon include *How to be a Successful Secretary* and *Changing Course: How to take charge of your career* (both with with Stephen Hoare) and *A Weight Off Your Mind: How to stop worrying about your body size*

D1122799

Overcoming Common Problems Series

For a full list of titles please contact
Sheldon Press, Marylebone Road, London NW1 4DU

Beating Job Burnout
DR DONALD SCOTT

Beating the Blues
SUSAN TANNER AND JILLIAN
BALL

Being the Boss
STEPHEN FITZSIMON

Birth Over Thirty
SHEILA KITZINGER

Body Language
How to read others' thoughts by their
gestures
ALLAN PEASE

Bodypower
DR VERNON COLEMAN

Bodysense
DR VERNON COLEMAN

Calm Down
How to cope with frustration and anger
DR PAUL HAUCK

Changing Course
How to take charge of your career
SUE DYSON AND STEPHEN HOARE

Comfort for Depression
JANET HORWOOD

Complete Public Speaker
GYLES BRANDRETH

**Coping Successfully with Your Child's
Asthma**
DR PAUL CARSON

**Coping Successfully with Your Hyperactive
Child**
DR PAUL CARSON

**Coping Successfully with Your Irritable
Bowel**
ROSEMARY NICOL

Coping with Anxiety and Depression
SHIRLEY TRICKETT

Coping with Blushing
DR ROBERT EDELMANN

Coping with Cot Death
SARAH MURPHY

Coping with Depression and Elation
DR PATRICK McKEON

Coping with Stress
DR GEORGIA WITKIN-LANOIL

Coping with Suicide
DR DONALD SCOTT

Coping with Thrush
CAROLINE CLAYTON

Curing Arthritis – The Drug-Free Way
MARGARET HILLS

Curing Arthritis Diet Book
MARGARET HILLS

**Curing Coughs, Colds and Flu – The
Drug-Free Way**
MARGARET HILLS

Curing Illness – The Drug-Free Way
MARGARET HILLS

Depression
DR PAUL HAUCK

Divorce and Separation
ANGELA WILLANS

Don't Blame Me!
How to stop blaming yourself
and other people
TONY GOUGH

The Epilepsy Handbook
SHELAGH McGOVERN

**Everything You Need to Know about
Adoption**
MAGGIE JONES

**Everything You Need to Know about
Contact Lenses**
DR ROBERT YOUNGSON

**Everything You Need to Know about
Osteoporosis**
ROSEMARY NICOL

Overcoming Common Problems Series

Overcoming Common Problems Series

Hysterectomy
SUZIE HAYMAN

Jealousy
DR PAUL HAUCK

Learning from Experience
A woman's guide to getting
older without panic
PATRICIA O'BRIEN

Learning to Live with Multiple Sclerosis
DR ROBERT POVEY, ROBIN DOWIE
AND GILLIAN PRETT

Living Alone – A Woman's Guide
LIZ McNEILL TAYLOR

Living Through Personal Crisis
ANN KAISER STEARNS

Living with Grief
DR TONY LAKE

Living with High Blood Pressure
DR TOM SMITH

Loneliness
DR TONY LAKE

Making Marriage Work
DR PAUL HAUCK

Making the Most of Loving
GILL COX AND SHEILA DAINOW

Making the Most of Yourself
GILL COX AND SHEILA DAINOW

Managing Two Careers
How to survive as a working mother
PATRICIA O'BRIEN

Meeting People is Fun
How to overcome shyness
DR PHYLLIS SHAW

Menopause
RAEWYN MACKENZIE

The Nervous Person's Companion
DR KENNETH HAMBLY

Overcoming Fears and Phobias
DR TONY WHITEHEAD

Overcoming Shyness
A woman's guide
DIANNE DOUBTFIRE

Overcoming Stress
DR VERNON COLEMAN

Overcoming Tension
DR KENNETH HAMBLY

Overcoming Your Nerves
DR TONY LAKE

The Parkinson's Disease Handbook
DR RICHARD GODWIN-AUSTEN

Say When!
Everything a woman needs to know about
alcohol and drinking problems
ROSEMARY KENT

Self-Help for your Arthritis
EDNA PEMBLE

Slay Your Own Dragons
How women can overcome
self-sabotage in love and work
NANCY GOOD

Sleep Like a Dream – The Drug-Free Way
ROSEMARY NICOL

Solving your Personal Problems
PETER HONEY

A Special Child in the Family
Living with your sick or disabled child
DIANA KIMPTON

Think Your Way to Happiness
DR WINDY DRYDEN AND JACK GORDON

Trying to Have a Baby?
Overcoming infertility and child loss
MAGGIE JONES

Why Be Afraid?
How to overcome your fears
DR PAUL HAUCK

Women and Depression
A practical self-help guide
DEIDRE SANDERS

You and Your Varicose Veins
DR PATRICIA GILBERT

Your Arthritic Hip and You
GEORGE TARGET

Your Grandchild and You
ROSEMARY WELLS

Overcoming Common Problems

COPING SUCCESSFULLY WITH MIGRAINE

Sue Dyson

SHELDON PRESS
LONDON

First published in Great Britain in 1991
Sheldon Press, SPCK, Marylebone Road, London NW1 4DU

© Sue Dyson 1991

All rights reserved. No part of this book may be reproduced
or transmitted in any form or by any means, electronic or
mechanical, including photocopying, recording, or by any
information storage and retrieval system, without permission
in writing from the publisher.

British Library Cataloguing in Publication Data
Dyson, Sue
  Coping successfully with migraine.
  1. Migraine. Therapy
  I. Title
  616.85706

ISBN 0–85969–626–X

Photoset by Deltatype Ltd, Ellesmere Port, Cheshire
Printed in Great Britain by Biddles Ltd, Guildford and Kings Lynn

Contents

Preface
by Dr Anne MacGregor

'There is no justice in migraine' writes Sue Dyson in this book. Throughout history, people from all walks of life have suffered from the affliction. Many may not even know that the blinding headaches which seem to come 'out of the blue' with irritating regularity are in fact migraine headaches. It is wrongly thought that people with migraine see 'flashing lights' before the headaches. In fact, the majority of migraine sufferers have no such a warning before an attack.

All too often sufferers try and keep their agony to themselves in the mistaken belief that 'nothing can be done'. How wrong they could be. Even if your own family doctor does not have an interest in migraine, there are now specialist clinics where headache sufferers can be referred for treatment and advice. Many neurology clinics in main hospitals have doctors working there who have an interest in migraine. Within the last decade, groups of doctors have formed societies devoted to the study of headache. International meetings are held where doctors present the findings of their research. Several specialist medical journals are now published, presenting papers on headache. Major drug companies are undertaking extensive research with the aim of finding an effective treatment for migraine attacks and broadening our understanding of the condition. . . . The list goes on.

Even with all this international interest in headache, there is, as yet, no cure. Drug treatment is certainly necessary to help gain early relief and in some cases, to reduce the frequency of attacks. However, research has shown is that much can be done by the migraine sufferer to help themselves. This is what this book is all about. Read carefully – it may even put me out of a job!

Dr Anne MacGregor
The City of London Migraine Clinic

1

Migraine and Everyday Life

Anyone who has ever suffered from migraine will be only too aware of the effects of the illness on daily life. According to the National Headache Foundation – an American organization set up to help migraine and other headache sufferers – American industry lost around $50 billion from absenteeism and medical expenses in 1989, all linked to headache pain. In fact, headaches accounted for around 157 million lost working days during the same period.

But we are not just talking about inconvenience and economic difficulties; the cost in terms of individual suffering is infinitely higher. Apart from the practical problems they face, sufferers and their friends and families are often in a state of anxiety and bewilderment, particularly in the days following initial diagnosis.

This chapter is intended to help anyone for whom migraine is a new experience – by explaining what happens, what to expect and by showing that you are definitely not alone. We shall then move on to discuss some of the positive measures you can take to fight back!

There is no doubt at all that migraine has a significant effect upon the daily lives of all sufferers and their families. Even those who suffer mild and infrequent attacks – and try to carry on their lives regardless –admit that the quality of life is diminished during attacks. For those sufferers who live with migraine on an almost daily basis, life can become almost unbearable. Indeed, in some (thankfully rare) cases, sufferers have become so depressed and overwhelmed by it that they have had to give up their jobs; a few have even attempted suicide. This sad fact is made even more tragic by the fact that their despair was unnecessary: all sufferers can be helped significantly, by a combination of therapies, changes in lifestyle, and sympathetic and practical support from others.

This book aims to help you to live with your migraine, and – if at all possible – to conquer it or to rise above it. But in order to do so, other people's attitudes have to be changed: after all, stress is a major factor in migraine, and the hostility or apparent indifference of family and friends can place enormous stress upon the sufferer.

This chapter contains accounts by sufferers. These people explain what they feel far better than any medical textbook, and I hope that they will help you to understand and empathize with some of the

1

feelings and experiences which are so difficult for sufferers to express.

The aim of it all, of course, is greater understanding: both by fellow-sufferers and by their friends and families who have never had to walk through the dark gate into the lonely world of migraine.

Physical feelings

Some migraine sufferers know instinctively when they are going to have an attack. Others can be taught to recognize the early warning signs once they know what to look for: a certain food, perhaps, flickering light, or the internal warning-signs.

Classical migraine sufferers have the most easily recognizable early warning signs, called the 'aura': Philip is in his late 50s and has suffered from classical migraine for many years. For him, the aura is the most distressing part of the attack, as his headaches are not very severe.

Jean is 51 and also suffers from migraine, but her warning symptoms are rather different from Philip's as she does not suffer from aura. One of her main symptoms is a general feeling of unease, which can be tempting to ignore. Another interesting warning sign is a personality change: she finds herself eating and talking very quickly – and her family have learned to recognize this, as Jean herself is less likely to acknowledge it. She also craves sweet foods (honey sandwiches and Horlicks) which seem to relieve the pain.

Adrienne gives the following account of one of her migraine attacks:

I awake about 3 am, with a heavy pressure on the top of my head. I take paracetamol, which helps me to go back to sleep. But I awake again about 5 or 6 am, feeling no different at all. I get up with slightly blurred vision, like my head is full of water, or I have a net curtain in front of my eyes. I have a nasty taste in my mouth, which lasts for the three days of a migraine attack.

The pain gets gradually worse. I seem to go to the toilet more frequently, often the eye where the pain is worse keeps watering, and my nose runs. The pain often feels as if there is a rusty vice clamped around my head or a steel stake going through it. I just long to lay down and close my eyes, but I can't sleep because the pain is too bad. I am often sick.

On the second day, I awake feeling wretched. I want to sleep, but have to get up as I have a large family. Sometimes around midday it goes off a bit, but I feel very dazed, tired and not myself at all. I go to bed as early in the evening as I am able. But a few hours later, I awake with the wretched intense pain again. When I get up in the morning, it's unbearable.

On day three, the pain is so bad that I feel I am surely going to die. I feel my head is going to burst open. I feel as if blood is going to come out of my eyes, as if my head will explode. I feel this dreadful pain will never go, but by about 11 am I can feel it starting to lift. By noon I am feeling so much better. When at last it goes, I feel like a new person. I feel on a high. I can dance and sing and be nice to everyone I meet.

During an attack, physical feelings can vary enormously. Some people have very brief, mild attacks, which they can work through and appear outwardly normal. Not every migraine attack involves headache, and some sufferers have only the neurological symptoms – the aura: this is called a 'migraine aura without headache', previously known as 'migraine equivalent'.

Mind you, the aura symptoms in themselves can be very unpleasant, and some sufferers fear them even more than the headache. They may be accompanied by nausea and disorientation, and new or undiagnosed sufferers are sometimes afraid that they herald some dreadful illness, such as a brain tumour or a stroke.

The headache varies in severity, and most sufferers find that they have different types of attack at different times in their lives. At their worst, migraine headaches are excruciating and it is impossible to concentrate on anything else. The world is the pain, and the pain is the world; nothing else exists. It is impossible to work, or talk, or do anything but wait for the pain to go away.

The pain is usually behind one eye, though not every migraine headache is so localized or one-sided. Often it throbs with every beat of the heart. The physical disturbance of vomiting makes the throbbing worse, but after a few minutes the headache may subside a little, temporarily or permanently.

Most sufferers cannot bear bright light, loud noises or strong smells. Many suffer nausea and vomiting and whilst some cannot eat anything, others want to eat even though they feel sick.

Practical implications

Anyone who suffers from moderate or severe migraine has to learn to adapt his or her life to fit in with the attacks. Some find that they can steel themselves to get through a working day or a trying time, but that immediately afterwards they have to collapse and tell the world to go away. For those who cannot stave off the migraine in this way, an attack means an immediate and complete interruption of the daily routine. Going to the shops, going to work, talking to people, even enjoyable things like going to a party – all these things are out of the question during an attack, because they would cause immense stress and suffering.

Then there is the problem of drugs – of always having to carry them with you, and perhaps having to ask for glasses of water at inconvenient moments. Worse, if you have an attack and you need to lie down somewhere quiet, it's going to be a problem if you're in the middle of Oxford Street on Christmas Eve!

Some sufferers do not drive, because they are worried about the effect which their migraine might have on them as drivers. First, there is the question of the pre-headache aura, which can be quite disorientating and which may disrupt vision and co-ordination so badly that the sufferer actually becomes a danger on the road. Second, there is the problem of being stranded somewhere and unable to drive back home. Many sufferers – including Jean – have earned parking-tickets because they had to go and sit somewhere quiet, instead of driving home on time.

There are also many leisure activities which some sufferers feel they cannot participate in for fear of precipitating an attack: vigorous exercise, walking in windy or very sunny conditions, disco-dancing, and even visits to a restaurant or friends – all can bring on attacks in some people.

Jean used to work for someone else, but has now turned to self-employment because it is more flexible. Yet self-employment is not the perfect solution, as she explains:

After being a teacher, I am now self-employed, selling antiques at fairs. At all these times, migraine has been a real curse, and particularly now I am self-employed the hours wasted when so much polishing etc. needs doing are so frustrating. People who say they just work on through a headache don't know what they are talking about! There are times when I am halfway down the M1

4

with a car full of stock, *en route* for a fair, when I *have* to sit and die quietly in a corner of a Little Chef until my senses recover enough to continue. But on such occasions I feel like a wet rag for days after.

Knowing that bed, sleep and quiet are the best answers does not help when you are in the middle of a town full of Christmas shoppers, or in a hotel with all my stock set out, customers asking questions, and the prospect of having to pack it all up and drive home. But these are times when you draw upon hidden resources of energy and determination merely to survive: having a fit of the vapours doesn't solve anything. I'm sure I must be quite rude to people at such times.

Other people's attitudes

If there is one great universal truth about migraine, it is this: you can't really appreciate what it's like until you've had it yourself.

The invisibility of migraine (no lumps, bumps or plaster-casts) makes it easy to fake and easy to dismiss as 'just a headache'. Colleagues who habitually take days off sick with phoney migraine attacks are generally the people who have never had a real attack in their lives. Obviously, this is very upsetting for someone who really is suffering – when the phoney sufferer strolls in to work the next day, full of the joys of spring, it just serves to trivialize migraine even more in the eyes of bosses and workmates. Pretty soon, anyone with migraine is suspected of malingering. As Dr Anne MacGregor observes: 'People sometimes end up ringing work and saying they've got 'flu instead, because they're ashamed. There's a lack of understanding about how different migraine is from a headache. Sufferers begin to feel guilty about themselves.'

Migraine is a very inconvenient illness, and sometimes it descends at the worst possible moment – just when you really can't afford to let the side down. The trouble is, that worrying about an approaching event can actually bring on an attack: if family and friends keep reminding you not to be ill on such-and-such an occasion they are in fact only making it more likely that you *will* be ill!

Equally distressing are other people's attitudes: they can turn an inconvenient and unpleasant illness into sheer torture. An unsympathetic or hostile attitude not only makes the sufferer feel guilty and inferior, but the tension tends to make the physical symptoms worse. On the other hand, the attitude of a colleague who understands what you are going through can bring enormous relief from the cycle of guilt and inadequacy – and freedom from stress can often bring some relief of physical symptoms.

Psychological and emotional effects

The physical, the emotional and the practical are all very tightly bound together in migraine. For some sufferers, a feeling of tension or guilt or inadequacy is enough in itself to bring on an attack. The attack, in turn, provokes more feelings of tension, guilt and inadequacy – and so the vicious circle goes on.

It is hard to say 'I give in' and go to bed, when you know that your work colleagues or friends are thinking 'What a wimp', or 'It's just an excuse for another afternoon off'. But there are always times when the pain and suffering are too bad *not* to give in.

In severe cases, sufferers may, in effect, withdraw from society altogether, simply to avoid potentially stressful situations which might trigger an attack. One common fear is of being ill in someone else's house – far from the warmth and peaceful darkness of your own bedroom – especially if the people you are staying with do not have a sympathetic understanding of your problem.

The effects of successful treatment

The sudden discovery of a successful treatment, or the natural cessation of attacks, e.g. at the menopause, can have a truly miraculous effect on a sufferer. At first there may be caution, even suspicion: 'Is this really happening?' 'Is it just a placebo effect?' 'Am I imagining this?' 'Will it all begin again, as soon as I start taking life for granted?' And then there will be joy, elation, tears of relief – for being released from the endless treadmill of migraine is just as emotional an experience as being released from a dark and lonely prison cell.

There are hundreds of thousands of people in this country who can be helped by migraine therapies – both conventional and 'alternative'; there are very few who cannot be helped at all. Therefore if one particular treatment doesn't work it makes very good sense to try and try again, until something does. Even a slight improvement can make a big difference to your life. Every migraine sufferer is *different*. What works for one person may not work for you – but if you don't try it, you'll never know!

If you are the relative, friend, or colleague of a migraine sufferer, you probably care very deeply but feel there is little you can do to help. This simply isn't so. In the next chapter, we look at the many ways in which you can help both the sufferer and yourself to feel better and much more in control.

Summing up

- Migraine isn't just a physical problem: it also has psychological and practical implications for the daily lives of sufferers.
- You are not alone in feeling afraid or guilty about your migraine. But if you can eliminate these negative feelings and approach life in a more positive way, you may well obtain real physical benefits too.
- Don't deny yourself the right to skilled medical help: successful treatment can transform your life.

2

Why Me? Migraine:
Who Gets It and Why

Perhaps your doctor has just told you that you are suffering from migraine; or perhaps you have a close friend or relative who is a sufferer. Either way, the chances are that you are feeling confused and not too sure about exactly what you are dealing with.

The symptoms of migraine have been recognized for thousands of years – as early as 400 BC – and there have been many famous sufferers, including Julius Caesar, Charles Darwin, Lewis Carroll and Sigmund Freud. Despite being a very common illness, migraine has not always been understood or handled sympathetically. There are many myths and old wives' tales about migraine, perhaps because scientists know relatively little about what a migraine is, what happens during an attack, and why some get it and the rest of us don't.

What is migraine?

As yet, little is known for certain about migraine. Serious research has only been under way for a century or so, and it is only in the last 50 years that we have had any effective forms of treatment. So, the process of finding a cure is still in its infancy.

Scientists describe migraine as a 'vascular headache' – that is, that the headache involves changes in the behaviour of the blood vessels. It has been suspected for many years that before an attack the vessels around the brain become constricted (narrowed), and then dilate (expand) to much more than their normal size. It is in this phase of dilation that the headache is felt. It is usually one-sided, and may feel as though it is throbbing in time with the pulse: each beat of the heart pumps more blood into the already-congested blood vessels of the head, causing more pain.

It used to be thought that it was this unusual activity in the blood vessels which actually caused a migraine attack, but nowadays most doctors believe that this is only a symptom – a result of much more complex changes in the brain itself.

The 'neurological' theory favoured at present by most specialists propounds that migraine involves important chemical changes in the brain, affecting the activity of nerves (which carry messages about sensations like pain). Experiments have shown that a sort of wave of inactivity (called a 'nerve storm') may pass over the surface of the brain just before an attack. One of the chemicals thought to be involved is serotonin, the levels of which seem to fall during an attack. Serotonin is associated with constriction of the blood vessels and has an action in an area in the brainstem, the part of the brain at the top of the spine which stops us feeling pain. Doctors talk about a 'pain gate', which is normally kept 'closed' by the brainstem, so that we don't suffer pain. It is when chemical changes leave the pain gate open that we are likely to suffer migraine attacks. Anxiety seems to open the pain gate, whereas relaxation techniques can be used to help close it – one reason why migraine sufferers often find relaxation useful.

It is now believed that, in order for an attack to begin, a combination of several factors (or 'triggers') has to be at work. For example, even if you tend to be sensitive to cheese, it may be that you will not get a fullblown migraine attack unless you are also under stress or approaching a menstrual period or drinking cheap red wine. Trigger factors vary between people, which is why the approach to treatment must also vary according to the individual and his or her lifestyle.

One simple piece of advice: pain protects the body from further injury. A migraine attack could be your body's way of making you stop and switch off when you have been overdoing it.

Different types of migraine

One of the characteristics of migraine which makes it so difficult to treat is the fact that it varies so much between individuals. There are, in fact, almost as many varieties of migraine as there are individual sufferers. Nevertheless, several distinct types are recognized by doctors:

Migraine without aura (previously called 'common migraine')

This is the type of migraine which most people (90%) suffer from. It is more than merely 'a headache'. The National Headache Foundation in America describes common migraine as:

> Severe, one-sided throbbing pain, often accompanied by nausea, vomiting, cold hands, tremor, dizziness, sensitivity to sound and light.

9

In common migraine, the severe, one-sided headache often comes on without warning. Like all types of migraine, it may come on at regular intervals (say, once a week or once a month), or in response to a particular set of circumstances and/or stimuli (e.g. foods, environmental factors, stress etc).

Case study Joy is 59 and has suffered from common migraine for about 25 years. Her attacks come on at regular intervals – either monthly or fortnightly – and especially at weekends. She has no warning of an attack: 'just a sudden headache over one eye, or the back of the head, plus feeling sick'.

Joy has a stressful job, and feels that her attacks tend to come on after stress, rather than during it. In the past, this meant many cancelled social arrangements and ruined weekends. She has since found relief through transcendental meditation.

Migraine with aura (previously called 'classical migraine')

Like common migraine sufferers, those affected by classical migraine have a powerful, one-sided headache with nausea and vomiting, dislike of strong light, loud noises and pungent smells.

The difference between common and classical migraine lies in what doctors call the aura: the set of internal warning signs which tell the

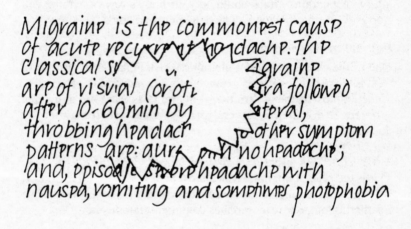

Figure 1. Visual representation of one type of aura
© Dr Anne MacGregor

sufferer that an attack is on the way. The aura varies widely between sufferers, but generally lasts between a few minutes and one hour, and usually stops when the headache starts. This is the preheadache stage that has been associated with constricted blood vessels in the head.

It is important to recognize that the migraine attack does not consist simply of the headache phase: it also includes any early warning signs (the 'prodromes') the aura and any after-effects such as feeling 'washed-out' (the 'postdromes'). The body prepares itself for the attack long before the headache begins, and this is why early treatment is important to control attacks.

Aura symptoms may include one or more of the following:

- visual disturbances: flashing lights, spots, zig-zags, coloured stars etc; sometimes blind spots or even complete temporary loss of vision; double vision
- pins and needles, weakness or numbness in the arms or legs (especially the hands and feet, and usually on one side); in rare cases, there may even be temporary paralysis

Other symptoms which you may notice include:

- blurred vision (can occur during attack also)
- changes in the perception of objects, the world, other people, and even the self (known as the 'Alice in Wonderland syndrome'; can be prodromal)
- slurred speech, or difficulty in expressing one's thoughts (often remains during attack
- heightened sense of smell (usually part of attack)
- nasty taste in mouth (usually part of attack)

Case study Philip is 57, and has suffered from classical migraine since he was a boy. His father also suffered from it, as Philip recalls:

I seem to have inherited my susceptibility to these attacks from my father. He used to complain that he could see only half of everything he looked at.

My own migraine attacks generally occur at quite long intervals. Each attack evolves through three identifiable phases. First, the left half of every object I look at disappears, the impairment of vision being equal in both eyes. Second, a thin, horizontal band of throbbing light appears, which expands (in bad attacks) to cover a large area of my field of vision with bright zig-zag patterns. Third, the pain begins to intensify, seeming to be concentrated in the right side of the forehead and right temple, and this pain continues for a while after the vibrating patterns have faded away – usually within the hour.

I have found that my speech is less lucid before and during my attacks. Also, any writing done before, during or very soon after an attack displays unusual blemishes – for example, I sometimes miss out the final letters of words.

Aura symptoms may be alarming, but they are not at all dangerous. They are probably a result of chemical changes in the brain, but they do not harm the brain in any way. Some people have even found the aura a source of artistic inspiration for poems, pictures, novels etc: Lewis Carroll was a sufferer, and it has been suggested that his slowly disappearing Cheshire Cat was based on visual disturbances similar to those which some people experience prior to classical migraine attacks. In recent years, an international Migraine Art competition has allowed sufferers to externalize their aura symptoms and emotions by expressing them in picture form: an excellent way of showing sufferers that they are not alone, and of expressing the pain and confusion of migraine for the benefit of those who have never suffered from it.

As well as these aura-symptoms, there may be even earlier prodromes (warning signs), often the previous day. It is worth asking your family and friends to note down any changes they may notice in your moods etc, as these may help you to pinpoint the times when you are likely to have an attack. Signs may include:

– strange sensations
– hunger, thirst or food cravings
– mood changes, e.g. feeling low, anxiety, elation (these may be very subtle)
– feeling full of energy (as if you'll never have another attack)
– lassitude
– premonitions
– yawning

Brian – a migraine sufferer since his schooldays – finds that his wife is better able to spot one of his impending attacks than he is!

My wife notices that the day before a very severe attack, I am particularly well, gregarious and happy. My wife has noted this in her diary and there is a definite indication of this pattern.

Prodromes do not mean classical migraine is diagnosed unless the aura is present. Prodromes may also precede attacks of common migraine.

During an attack

During the acute phase of an attack, most common and classical migraine sufferers find that all they want to do is to lie (or sit) quietly, in the dark, and try to sleep, though some sufferers say that in mild attacks they prefer to 'keep going', as this tends to make the attack go away more quickly. In their experience, the pain seems to bother them more when they 'give in' to it than when they grit their teeth and keep going.

Apart from the headache and sickness (some sufferers may want to eat in spite of feeling nauseous), other migraine symptoms may include:

- sensitivity to light: the most common symptoms after headache and nausea
- diarrhoea
- frequent urination or fluid retention
- feeling very hot or very cold
- heightened sensitivity to sounds, smells (smells may aggravate headaches)
- speech problems
- general malaise

Other types of migraine

Migraine aura without headache, previously called 'migraine equivalents'

Strange though it may seem, not all migraine sufferers get headaches! Or, to be more specific, not all migraine attacks involve headache pain. Attacks like this are called migraine equivalents.

In this case, the sufferer has only the aura – and not the headache which usually follows. Although this may sound like a distinct improvement on the full-blown classical attack, many sufferers say that they find the aura symptoms distressing in themselves.

Cluster headache

As mentioned in the previous chapter, cluster headache is not really a form of migraine, yet it is often grouped together with migraine.

This form of excruciatingly painful headache comes in 'clusters' lasting 6–12 weeks, and there can be several attacks a day. Sufferers feel the need to move around during attacks, often pacing up and down and hitting their heads against the wall. Migraine sufferers, on the other hand, prefer to remain still.

Although cluster headache tends to be associated with middle-aged men who have smoked, there are also many female sufferers. Alcohol may trigger an attack but only in the cluster period and not at other times. The pain affects one eye only, which goes red and waters. The same nostril also waters and the other side of the face is unaffected.

Case study Felix is 38, and has suffered from cluster headaches for 11 years. Until last year, he had daily attacks and had reached the point of desperation – but hospitalization and experiments with various different drugs has now succeeded in reducing his headaches to manageable proportions. He is also able to help himself with various home remedies and coping strategies.

Felix's attacks come on suddenly: 'They may start with a pain under the eyes, but normally the nostrils block up (like the start of a cold), there is an excruciating pain in the left eye only, which waters and runs down the face. The eye also becomes smaller.'

Mixed and combination headaches

Although we have looked at types of migraine and non-migraine headache separately, it would be a mistake to assume that each type is mutually exclusive.

Although most sufferers get either common migraine or classical migraine, it is perfectly possible to suffer from both types, and some people suddenly switch from one form to the other for no apparent reason. Many sufferers also alternate between migraine headaches and muscle tension headaches, sometimes experiencing 'mixed' attacks with features of both conditions.

In fact, Dr Anne MacGregor, of the City of London Migraine

Clinic, notes that: 'We tend not to see patients until they have developed mixed headaches: they can cope with the migraine by itself, but when they start getting other headaches as well, it's just too much to bear.'

If you are a chronic headache sufferer, you may well find that your headaches do not always follow the same pattern. Sometimes they are like straightforward migraine attacks, whereas at other times they are more like tension headaches. Sometimes one form of attack may merge into another.

Because of this close inter-relation between different types of head pain, there are a few experts who claim that there is no such thing as migraine, only headache. A headache is a headache, they believe and it is a mistake to try to distinguish between different types.

Nevertheless, most migraine sufferers – and especially classical migraine sufferers – are only too aware of the difference between their migraine attacks and any other headaches they may suffer from time to time.

After the attack (the 'postdromal' stage)

Headaches vary tremendously in length, from a brief, sharp pain to the day-in, day-out burden of chronic tension headache.

Most migraine attacks last between 2–3 hours and 3 days. Some people manage to keep going during an attack, but for many sufferers the only possible course of action is lying down in a darkened room and trying to sleep – sleep often helps to shorten an attack.

After an attack, some sufferers find they are completely worn out – weak, exhausted, pale and incapable of doing anything much for hours or even days. Others have a very curious reaction to the attack: they emerge from the pain in a state of exhilaration and complete well-being, similar to the feelings which some people get before an attack. These sufferers may find that aborting an attack with drugs leaves them feeling vaguely ill for days on end, whereas allowing the attack to take its natural course gets it over with quickly and leaves them feeling happy and at peace with the world.

Obviously the decision to abort an attack or to go through with it ought to lie with the sufferer alone: but it is comforting to know that there is a medication to hand if things get unbearable. This is why it is so important to consult your doctor and obtain proper diagnosis and treatment. After all, you have just as much right to health and happiness as anyone else!

Who gets migraine?

Migraine knows no boundaries. It affects people from all walks of life, of all ages and both sexes. It does, however, follow certain identifiable patterns.

Children

Most childhood sufferers (around 80%) are boys – which is quite surprising since the majority of adult sufferers are female. No one has yet been able to explain this strange discrepancy, though it is usually linked to the trigger of hormonal changes in post-pubertal woman.

According to conventional medical theories, the commonest forms of migraine in childhood are common migraine and abdominal migraine, though some children suffer from classical migraine and also the rare but very distressing hemiplegic migraine.

Obviously it is difficult to explain to a child why he or she is suffering, and what is happening to his or her body. This is particularly true in relation to aura symptoms, which can be especially dramatic and upsetting for a child – giving rise to wild fantasies, 'visions' and fears of madness.

Dr Howard Freeman is a South London GP, and has also run a paediatric migraine clinic at Charing Cross Hospital for the last four years. Dr Freeman finds it difficult to accept some of the received wisdom about children and migraine, as the facts have simply not been borne out by his own experience of talking to young sufferers. For example, he questions the view that children's experiences of migraine are different from those of adults, believing that they in fact suffer from the same types of migraine – only finding it more difficult to express themselves because they are so young.

Patients – some as young as three – are referred to the clinic by their GPs. Dr Freeman feels that the clinic has a valuable role to play, both in confirming the GP's diagnosis, and in helping the doctors who work there to gain experience of working with children. It also fulfils an educational role, teaching parents to understand and help their children with migraine.

Dr Freeman's views on the subject of parents are quite controversial: 'I tend to think that a lot of children would not get migraine unless their parents gave it to them', he says, explaining that – as in adults – stress is the primary precipitating factor in most childhood cases of migraine, and the two major sources of that stress are home and school. Parents and schools can exert undue pressure upon children to conform, to do well and so on, and even suppress the child's personality. The resulting stress can trigger off childhood migraine.

Whilst accepting that food sensitivities can play a part in causing childhood migraine, Dr Freeman urges caution:

Many parents use food allergy to cover up the real reason for the migraine – parental pressures, for example. It's parental escapism. Often – with a child of say ten years old – I'll speak directly to the child, and the giveaway is when the parent answers! You see that right up to 13 or 14 year olds.

Some parents simply won't recognize it, and don't even come back to a second consultation. They won't accept that it could be due to their relationship with their child. They go to food allergists and alternative therapists, and spend a lot of money. Of course, migraine is cyclical, and if you go on long enough it will remit naturally. Also, as the child gets older and develops its own personality, the migraines will tend to remit. Then the parents will claim that the special diet has worked.

Dr Freeman is worried about the effect which obsessive diets may have upon young children:

I think it's unfair to children for parents to dictate these fashions for bizarre exclusion diets onto their children. In some cases, their diet may even be almost deprived – yet the parents go on with it, even when the headaches persist. My advice to parents would be: look to yourselves first of all for the cause. If you're not getting anywhere, seek skilled help and don't try to do it all on your own.

Apart from the question of stress, Dr Freeman highlights hormonal fluctuations as a trigger factor in childhood migraines: pointing out that the peak incidence among his patients is at puberty and around the time of GCSEs – both times when stress is high and hormones fluctuate wildly. A study at the City of London Migraine Clinic found that the peak of onset was at puberty and 10 years later: this again suggests that stress is an important factor.

As regards treatment, the paediatric migraine clinic concentrates on behavioural therapy rather than on drugs:

I am very reluctant to give long-term medication to children. You are looking at a long-term illness, and behavioural modification is the best course of action. So I recommend relaxation, parental education and for parents to discuss their child's migraine with schools. Schools are very, very bad at dealing with migraine, and are often actively hostile towards the child.

Although he implies that parental stress is high on the list of precipitating factors, Dr Freeman is quick to emphasize that he has great sympathy for any parent of a child who suffers from migraine:

Parents have all the problems of coping with a chronically sick child, and that's difficult. You don't want to make the child feel too different, but it nevertheless *is* different and you have to cope with that. Where parents go wrong is in seeing migraine not as a chronic illness, but as a series of one-off illnesses.

Some of Dr Freeman's young patients will grow up to be adult migraine sufferers; others will respond to treatment and become headache-free adults. Mercifully, most children can and do grow out of migraine and many of the others can be successfully treated with drugs or a combination of drugs and relaxation therapy. Dietary therapy has also had some success with children in trials, though – as Dr Freeman points out – the role of food sensitivities should not be exaggerated.

Dr Anne MacGregor also sees children at the City of London Migraine Clinic. She cites hypoglycaemia (low blood sugar) as a common precipitating factor in childhood migraine:

Poor diet, or not eating enough at the right times, can cause low blood sugar which in turn precipitates an attack. Or the migraine can be linked to a parent-child relationship. We have a child psychiatrist here, and we refer children to her right up to the age of 21.

Men

Only around one-fifth of all adult migraine sufferers are male, yet this still accounts for some two million suffering human beings, many of whom have to hold down responsible and stressful jobs even when they feel that they can cope no longer.

Admitting that they suffer from migraine is a very hard thing for some men to do. They are afraid that they will be thought of as weak, inadequate, unreliable. As a result, many sufferers may conceal their migraine as best they can, and miss out on the chance of effective medical treatment.

About 1% of people are cluster headache sufferers; three quarters of them men. This painful condition seems to affect especially men who are smokers, or who have smoked in the past.

Women

Women make up around two-thirds of all migraine sufferers, and this may be one reason why the disorder received relatively little attention from the medical profession until the proportion of female doctors and scientists began to increase in recent years.

Women tend to have different lifestyles and often more wide-ranging responsibilities than men. The challenge of bringing up a family, looking after a home and holding down a job can impose well-nigh intolerable stresses and strains on the most resilient of people, and stress always finds a way of manifesting itself in the end. In some women, the end result is migraine.

For others, causes of migraine include hormonal changes and postural problems which affect the equilibrium of the spine and the nerves and muscles which are attached to it.

Dr Anne MacGregor is a Registrar at the City of London Migraine Clinic, and a specialist in hormone-related migraine. Although many women come to her complaining of 'menstrual migraine', her own research suggests that true menstrual migraine – in which attacks happen around the first day of a period and at no other time – is relatively rare:

We undertook a study involving 100 women, around 50% of whom thought they had menstrually-related migraine, but when detailed records were kept over a period of months, it turned out that only three of the women fulfilled our strict criteria for menstrual migraine. However, a further 35% of women had an increased number of attacks at the time of their period, in addition to attacks at other times of the month.

On the other hand, Dr MacGregor is sure that hormones are a factor in precipitating attacks. In one study of 82 women, it turned out that eight of them had had their first migraine attack during the year of puberty, whilst a further seven reported that their migraine had started exactly ten years later.

No obvious links were found, for example, with a first pregnancy; but it seems likely that stress may have combined with the hormonal factors: puberty is a stressful time, and approximately ten years later many women are beginning their first responsible job, or getting married. Because migraine attacks have to result from a combination of factors, it may well be that this extra stress was a necessary element in triggering off the first attack.

Even when migraine does turn out to be menstrually related, Dr MacGregor is cautious about treating only the hormonal aspect of the problem:

There are so many changes in the body around that time. There are lower levels of endogenous opiates, for example, so you are more sensitive to pain. Migraine is always caused by a combination of factors, some of which it should be possible to eliminate. Many people find that eating small, frequent meals around the time of menstruation helps to maintain their blood sugar level and this in itself is enough to stave off an attack.

One curious fact which has emerged from Dr MacGregor's research is that there are fewer attacks related to menstruation among Roman Catholic women than among Anglicans.

An encouraging point is that many female migraine sufferers find that their migraine ceases during pregnancy and disappears altogether after the menopause – possibly because of hormonal changes. But some women still continue to have monthly migraines in spite of there being no hormonal fluctuations.

Although many women find that their migraine attacks improve or even disappear during pregnancy, it can sometimes trigger off a first attack, often with aura. In most cases, attacks will improve after the first three months of pregnancy. As a rule, drug therapy is not a very good idea during pregnancy. Dr Anne MacGregor recommends the following treatments:

– small, frequent meals
– rest
– paracetamol (if necessary)

If the vomiting is very severe, you should consult your GP and discuss whether further treatment is necessary.

The elderly

One good thing about being old is that your migraine is more likely to get better rather than worse. Most migraine sufferers (9 out of 10) have developed the condition by the time they are 40; the onset of migraine in the later years is very rare.

For those sufferers whose attacks do continue into their later years, there is some hope in the fact that many find the pain of the headache lessens as they get older, though attacks do tend to become more prolonged. The good news for women is that many of them find that their migraines get much better after the menopause.

A migraine personality?

It used to be thought that migraine sufferers shared certain identifiable personality traits: that they were obsessively tidy, conscientious, anxious people with above-average intelligence.

Modern medical thinking discounts this theory of a 'migraine personality', simply because research has not borne it out. It's true that there are some migraine sufferers who *are* highly-strung, obsessive intellectuals, but then again there are a lot more who aren't.

So, flattering though it may be to associate migraine with intelligence, it's much safer to conclude that migraine affects people of all ages, all classes, all personality types and both sexes. If migraine sufferers are sometimes anxious people, it is likely that this is the result of the pain, rather than the cause of it.

Why do people get migraine?

There is no single cause of migraine. It is not like catching 'flu, or breaking your leg. Migraine may come along quite suddenly, with no apparent reason, and then go away again just as suddenly and as inexplicably as it came.

This is, in fact, what happened to the wife of one famous Hollywood film star: for three miserable years, she suffered terrible and debilitating migraine attacks. Her husband felt powerless to help, though he did his best to make her more comfortable. Together, they visited every doctor and alternative therapist they could find. Nothing worked. And then, one day, the migraine went away and never came back – an enigma to the last.

There is no justice in migraine, and there are no hard and fast rules about who gets it and who doesn't. But there are recognizable patterns which suggest that some people are more at risk than others.

The important thing to remember is that one factor alone is unlikely to give you migraine; all the evidence points to attacks resulting from an 'explosive' combination of cause and circumstance. Some of the factors are unalterable and constant, but others are amenable to change. Therefore, removing some of the ingredients from the volatile mixture may help to deactivate your migraine before it gets a grip.

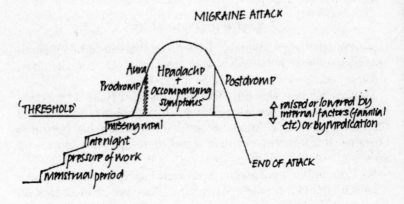

Figure 2. Diagram representing concept of requirement of spiral precipitating factors acting in combination to cross the 'threshold' of initiation of an attack of migraine.

© Dr Anne MacGregor

Common causes of migraine

Heredity

At least 10% of the population suffer from migraine, so it could be argued that – if we look hard enough – every one of us could find some obscure relative who was a migraine-sufferer. Indeed, research suggests that at least 60% of migraine sufferers seeking treatment have a *close* family history of migraine, so it seems reasonable to suppose that there may be a hereditary element in migraine.

There is another, more disturbing, side to this coin. Some researchers have suggested that – like other forms of behaviour – headache behaviour can be 'learned' from our parents. After all, we acquire many of our mannerisms and behaviour patterns from our parents, so why not this one too?

Dr Howard Freeman has noted manipulative behaviour in some of his young patients at the paediatric migraine clinic:

> A small percentage are displaying manipulative behaviour, often copied from the parents – and this is very difficult to treat. There may be a family history of the mother doing a 'dying duck' act every time she has a headache. This in turn is copied by the child, leading to the concept of heredity.

The problem is that it would be very difficult indeed for a parent who suffered from migraine to conceal that migraine from the children and try to behave 'normally', for their sake. Many parents already make heroic efforts to keep family life going, despite their sufferings; and it seems downright unreasonable to ask any more of them.

Perhaps it would be better not to try to conceal the migraine, but to learn ways of living with it successfully and positively. In this way, the parent provides a positive role model for the child who may in turn have to learn to live with migraine. If the child is also involved in carrying out these positive strategies, then he or she not only learns compassion, but also becomes accustomed to viewing migraine as a surmountable handicap rather than the end of the world.

On the positive side, at least having relatives who also suffer from migraine increases the likelihood that your own migraine will be well-understood and accepted without criticism, and that you will receive sympathetic and knowledgeable support from people who care about you.

Case study Sue is in her 30s. Her chances of not suffering from migraine were pretty slim from the start. Her mother and father both suffer from migraine-type headaches and her father also complains of a 'nervous stomach'. Both grandmothers suffered from severe migraine (though they preferred to talk about 'bilious attacks' or 'sick headaches').

Sue started having migraine as a small child, and her attacks have persisted to this day, although they have varied in frequency and intensity at different times of her life, e.g. during adolescence, times of extreme stress, and the days before a period. Luckily, she attended a specialist migraine clinic and now takes medication which reduces her attacks to manageable levels.

Sue is the author of this book.

Trigger factors

As we mentioned earlier on, migraine attacks are now believed to be the result of a combination of precipitating factors, called 'triggers'. Some triggers – like stress and certain foods – are well-known, but others may be quite rare or even unique. In the final analysis it is up to you to look at your lifestyle carefully and see if you can isolate some of the factors which contribute to your attacks. Remove one or more of the triggers, and you may be able to break the vicious circle once and for all.

Here are a few of the common triggers.

Food

Some people find that their migraine attacks are triggered by certain foods or food additives (and *lack* of food is also an important trigger – especially in young children). As we saw in the first chapter, many people who are not migraine sufferers get migraine-like vascular headaches when they eat some Chinese foods containing mono-sodium glutamate, processed meats containing nitrates or nitrites, or even cold foods like ice cream.

A relatively small number of migraine sufferers have genuine food sensitivities, although they do play a significant role in a many cases. It may be that you are only sensitive to one or two foods, for example. Also, women may find that they can eat a bar of chocolate or a piece of cheese most of the time without effect, but that around the time of a period the same food will trigger off an attack.

The following foods and drinks are known to precipitate migraine attacks in some people (a minority of sufferers):

- cheese (especially matured cheeses; cottage cheese and cream cheese tend to be all right)
- oranges and other citrus fruits
- alcohol, especially red wine, brandy and whisky (which contain high levels of additives called 'congeners')

- herrings
- chocolate
- vinegar and pickled foods
- smoked foods
- sour cream and yoghurt (some people are sensitive to all dairy products)
- nuts
- yeast
- wheat
- onions
- bananas
- pork
- caffeine (found in tea, coffee, cola drinks and chocolate)
- avocado
- foods containing nitrites and nitrates (e.g. hot dogs, salami)
- foods containing monosodium glutamate (avoid all processed foods unless you're sure they don't contain it – it gets into almost everything!)

Interestingly, a recent study at Charing Cross Hospital involving 60 migraine patients isolated the following foods as the most common culprits in causing attacks:

- wheat (found not just in bread, but in all flour-based products and also as a thickener, e.g. in soups)   78%
- oranges   65%
- eggs   45%
- tea and coffee   40%
- chocolate and milk   37%
- beef   35%
- corn, cane sugar and yeast   30%
- peas   28%

This is a very exhaustive list and it is highly unlikely that you would be sensitive to more than one or two of these foods – if any.

Many of these foods are not thought of as typical migraine triggers. So, the moral is, that you really have to monitor your own consumption and symptoms if you are going to be successful in eliminating your food triggers – if you have any. Not everybody does. It is important to remember that food is an important trigger for *some* people, and not important at all for others. Many migraine-sufferers deprive themselves unnecessarily of favourite foods: it's worth remembering La Rochefoucauld's maxim, 'To safeguard one's health at the cost of too strict a diet is a tiresome illness indeed'.

Obviously it would be dangerous to cut out large numbers of foods from your diet, especially all at once. You will not only be reducing its variety, but also damaging your nutritional intake. So, take advice from your doctor or eliminate only one food at a time, making a careful note of any effects. Chapter 3 contains advice on medically-supervised elimination diets, which can be used to identify food sensitivities. Specialists in food sensitivities and other environmental factors are called clinical ecologists and their work is discussed in Chapter 4 (The Alternative Approach) (See p. 61).

Dr Anne MacGregor emphasizes:

> People who suffer from true food intolerance are in a minority, yet this is a subject which is always focused on. Even if you are sensitive to some foods, it will only be a part of the problem. If you become obsessed with food sensitivity, you are just creating another extra illness, as well as isolating yourself socially.

Fasting

Some sufferers find that they get an attack if they miss a meal. This may be because they have become hypoglycaemic – i.e. their blood-sugar level has fallen to an unusually low level. Try to eat at regular times, and avoid sugary and fatty foods which may provoke violent swings in blood-sugar levels. Dietary suggestions are given in Chapter 7 (see p. 91). If you want to lose weight it is better and more effective to exercise regularly and eat sensibly than to skip meals.

Not just missing meals, but delayed meals or insufficient food can trigger attacks.

Smoking

Smoking is definitely a factor in the cause of some headaches – notably cluster headaches. One study showed that 53% of migraine sufferers who smoked became headache-free when they were asked to give up smoking and other migraine triggers, whereas only 13% of non-smokers became free from attacks when asked to give up trigger foods.

Stress

Many sufferers complain of migraine attacks not so much during periods of intense stress as immediately afterwards. It's as though the body copes for just long enough to get us over the crisis, and then lets us down with a bump. This is undoubtedly one of the reasons for the traditional 'Saturday-morning migraine', which has ruined many a well-earned break. (Though other reasons might include a delayed breakfast, sleeping-in, or even caffeine withdrawal.)

Chronic stress and anxiety can be just as bad. If your body is in a constant state of 'autonomic arousal', adrenaline and other stress by-products will build up in your body, and will tend to increase your muscle tension – which is itself a known factor in migraine – as well as producing further feelings of anxiety.

Migraine can be seen as a form of bodily 'power-cut', forcing us to shut down, give in and regain our forces before we face the stresses of daily life once again. Or it may be a 'cry for help'. Take the case of the lady whose husband was a chronic depressive with serious heart problems. Her migraine attacks were her way of getting back at his own illness – though she didn't want to admit that this was true. And although she tried all the treatments, nothing worked – because she didn't really want it to!

Research has indicated that relaxation techniques can be very effective in dealing with migraine: and some sample exercises, useful addresses and stress-reduction tips are given in Chapter 7. In some cases, clinical psychologists and psychotherapists can also help: your GP or migraine clinic will advise you.

Excitement

Excitement is a form of stress. No matter how enjoyable a situation may be, it can still be stressful, because it is placing unusual demands upon you and making you produce lots of adrenaline. When you come down from the 'high', the result may be a migraine.

But if you plan ahead and learn to relax properly, it is possible to have fun without fearing that you'll have to pay for it later.

Posture

Your head, neck and back are all joined together by your spine, so it is hardly surprising that if there is something wrong with your back, or if you are simply holding it badly, the result can be a headache. In fact, the whole of your skeleton is a finely poised framework; and if you don't learn to hold yourself in a relaxed and natural way, all sorts of things can go wrong. Tension is placed on muscles, and this in turn can irritate nerves and affect the flow of blood to the head. The net result may then be a tension headache and migraine.

Many types of work – e.g. sitting at a VDU writing this book! – can be conducive to migraine attacks because they encourage bad posture. So examining the way you stand and sit, and the chair you sit on, can be a good start. In some cases, special ergonomically designed chairs and beds can be a help, though they tend to be expensive.

Injuries can also cause problems, particularly injuries to the back, neck and shoulders – though migraine attacks caused by injury often settle down again once the injury has been treated. Pregnancy can also affect the spine and relax the ligaments, which can sometimes lead to injury.

For professional help with postural problems, consult an osteopath, a chiropractor, a physiotherapist or a teacher of the Alexander Technique (details in Chapter 4).

Sleep disturbance

Too much, or too little, sleep have been known to cause migraine attacks, as have any sudden change in your daily routine. Many sufferers, for example, find that they have attacks at the weekends, when they tend to have a 'lie-in'. If this is you, it's worth experimenting to see if getting up at your normal time will make any difference.

Hormonal changes

Fluctuations in hormonal levels, in female sufferers, can both improve and exacerbate migraine. Sometimes they can also trigger off a first attack. Common factors are pregnancy, the oral contraceptive pill (attacks often come during the pill-free week), the menopause and hormone replacement therapy.

Illness

Some sufferers find that their attacks are noticeably worse when they are at a 'low ebb', particularly when they are ill.

Environmental factors

Bright or flickering light, strong smells, stuffy rooms and fluorescent lighting can all trigger off attacks in some sufferers.

Keeping a migraine diary

The only reliable way to find out what causes your migraine is to keep a detailed 'migraine diary'.

This demands an organized approach and lots of commitment, because you have to keep it up day after day – even when you don't feel like it. A migraine diary should record all your physical and emotional feelings, plus what happens to you each day, what you eat and when, as well as detailing all your attacks and any treatment you take.

It's no good waiting until the end of the week and then trying to fill in the diary for the last seven days. We all have faulty memories, especially when we are asked to remember things we would rather forget, such as moments of extreme stress or pain. So it is vital that you commit yourself to completing your diary as a daily task. If you do so, it will be a help both to you and to your doctor in isolating 'trigger' factors, eliminating as many as possible, and finding new strategies and treatments.

It is also important to draw up your diary in a way which is easy for you to complete and easy to see the results. The best thing to do is to get an exercise-book or diary and rule up each page according to a set format. Or you could draw up a week's diary on a sheet of plain A4 paper, then make photocopies. The more user-friendly your diary is, the more you will want to use it.

Remember: the information you need to record is:

- day of the week, dates and times of attacks, stressful situations, etc
- how long each part of the attack lasted
- medication (regular preventive treatment and on-the-spot medication for attacks; prescription and over-the-counter remedies)
- home remedies and strategies, including alternative therapies
- possible triggers (e.g. foods, violent exercise, weather conditions)
- menstrual periods
- stressful situations: rate your stress level on a scale of 1 to 10, and *be honest*
- any pain (you can rate this on a scale of mild, moderate, severe)

Here is an example of a page from a migraine sufferer's diary,

1. Diary page showing migraine attacks

JULY Day	Headache pain	When started	Duration	Nausea/ vomiting	Medication	When taken	Possible triggers
1 Mon	SEVERE	2 pm	rest of day	YES	metaclom-pramide aspirin	2 pm 2 pm, 6 pm	cheese delayed lunch
2 Tues							
3 Wed							
4 Thurs							
5 Fri							
6 Sat	MODERATE	11 am	until late evening	NAUSEA	paracetamol	11 am, 3 pm	overslept ? hangover
7 Sun							
8 Mon							
9 Tues							

2. Diary page showing mixed headaches: ? analgesic-related headaches, plus one migraine attack

MAY Day	Headache pain	When started	Duration	Nausea/ vomiting	Medication	When taken	Possible triggers
1 Wed	MODERATE	7 am	all day	NO	paracetamol	7 am	got drunk the night before
2 Thurs	MILD	7 am	all day	NO	paracetamol	7 am, 1 pm	?
3 Fri	MILD	7·30 am	till late evening	NO	paracetamol	8 am	?
4 Sat	MODERATE	7 am	all day	NO	paracetamol	7 am	stressful day at work
5 Sun	MILD		all day	NO	No	—	?
6 Mon	SEVERE	10 am	all day	SEVERE	paracetamol	10 am, 2 pm	hangover ??
7 Tues	SEVERE	10 am	all day	SEVERE	too sick	—	
8 Wed	MILD	7 am	till 2 pm	NAUSEA	paracetamol	7 am	?
9 Thurs	NONE						

} POSSIBLE MIGRAINE ATTACK

Figure 3. Sample pages from Migraine Diaries

30

showing how this information could be set out. You can vary the layout to suit your own lifestyle and preferences, of course.

Summing up

- Migraine is much more than just a headache.
- There are two types of migraine: with and without aura.
- For a migraine attack to occur, several precipitating factors must be present: if you can eliminate some of these triggers, you may be able to prevent an attack occurring.
- There is always a headache-free period between attacks: a daily headache is not migraine.

3

Treating Your Migraine

All over the country, there are migraine sufferers who dismiss their illness with a brave smile and a shrug of the shoulders: 'I'm not really ill,' they say, 'not like people with real diseases . . . It's nothing serious, so I haven't seen the doctor – I just put up with it. Well that's life, isn't it?'

But that isn't life – or at least, it shouldn't be. It's hard to lead a full and satisfying life if you are dogged by insistent pain. Modern medicine recognizes the sufferings that migraine inflicts, and is making more and more of an effort to find drugs to help sufferers fight back.

Why you should see your doctor

Many of us are reluctant to go to the doctor: maybe we're worried about 'bothering' the GP with something so 'trivial'; maybe it's a fear of what the doctor might say; or maybe it's just the inconvenience of having to 'phone, making an appointment and then wait to be seen. When you're ill, you just can't face dragging yourself to the surgery; and when you're well, it's so easy to forget about your migraine altogether . . . until the next attack comes along.

There are plenty of reasons why you should see your doctor if you suffer from headaches; so if you have been putting it off for ages, perhaps you should cast an eye over this list:

- you might be worrying unnecessarily about something – a brain tumour, for example. If your fears turn out to be unfounded, you can stop worrying and get on with your life – and maybe the headaches will get better as a result.
- you may be suffering from a serious illness which requires immediate treatment.
- why should you suffer? The vast majority of headaches are treatable, and many are completely curable. It is your right to consult your doctor and ask for your pain to be treated.
- Migraine is no respecter of persons. There is nothing 'shameful' about admitting to headaches. Headache pain is a severe problem for millions of people.

The rule is, *always consult your doctor if you are worried*, or if:

- You suddenly start getting headaches
- Headache follows a head injury
- A temperature, or other symptoms like nausea and dislike of light accompany the headache(s)
- There is constant or frequent pain
- The nature of your headaches changes without any obvious reason.

Helping your doctor to help you

The trouble with migraine headaches is that when you have an acute attack, you feel so terrible that the last thing you want to do is go to the doctor, even though you are desperate for relief. You may also feel that, since you have 'only got a headache', you are not ill enough to justify calling the doctor out.

Once the attack is gone and you feel human again, it's tempting to forget all about the pain and to convince yourself that you won't have another attack. On the other hand, if you *do* go to see the doctor, you may feel like a fraud – and it can be difficult and uncomfortable to recall distressing symptoms when you don't actually feel ill.

Because headaches are a feature of so many different disorders, your GP may not be able to provide an on-the-spot diagnosis of your particular problem. As we have seen, even the diagnosis of migraine can be complicated if the sufferer has 'mixed' headaches.

It will help your doctor a great deal if you do some preparation before you go to the surgery. If you have been keeping a 'migraine diary', bring it with you. In order to make an accurate diagnosis, the GP needs to have the following information:

- how long have you had the headaches?
- what is the 'history' of your headaches?
- what are your symptoms?
- which factors do you think might be bringing on the headaches?
- how is your lifestyle (including any problems or exceptional stress)?
- what (if any) medicines are you taking?
- what medication or other treatments (including 'alternative' medicines) have you taken in the past?

Patients often find it difficult to talk to doctors, as though they were afraid of wasting his or her time. It's important that you don't feel intimidated; if you do, perhaps you should consider changing your GP.

Remember though that your GP cannot know how you feel if you are not open and informative. It may help to take along a friend or relative who knows what you have been going through, and who may be able to help out with the description of your attacks, or to 'rehearse' what you want to say to your doctor beforehand. The best way of making sure that you provide all the information is to write it down: when we feel nervous or rushed, we sometimes forget what we wanted to say and may miss out something important.

Be careful not to underestimate the severity of your symptoms, or to belittle your suffering as this will only give the doctor a false picture of your problem. It is all too easy to say something like 'I'm sorry to bother you, doctor, but it's these headaches. Oh, they're not too bad really . . .', when the truth of the matter is that you are in agony and reaching the end of your tether. Don't be ashamed of being honest.

Once your doctor has talked to you about your headaches, you may be asked to provide more detailed information before a final diagnosis can be made: and this is where a headache diary can come into its own. It requires commitment, but can be very helpful in revealing patterns of cause and effect, and bringing to light possible trigger factors.

It is possible that your GP may also decide to carry out some tests to make sure that you are not suffering from a serious illness. (Don't worry about this daunting list of tests: in most cases, the symptoms of migraine will be obvious to the doctor, and you won't need any of these additional tests. But equally, don't be afraid to ask what the tests are for.) Tests may include:

– blood test
– eye test
– brain scan
– neck X-ray
– lumbar puncture
– X-ray of sinuses

Dr Anne MacGregor, of the City of London Migraine Clinic, stresses the importance of a two-way flow of information between doctor and patient, and the need for the patient to feel involved in his or her own treatment:

> I always try to explain as much as possible about migraine to the patient: why it's happening, how the drugs work, and why it's so important to take them early. This puts responsibility back into the patient's hands. I try to open up that side of things, rather than just dictate what patients should do. I say: go away and record your headaches for three months. See how many trigger factors you can identify. See what treatment you find works for you and what doesn't. Come back and we'll discuss all these things. It's a two-way flow.

Certainly you should never accept anything you are unhappy with, or be afraid to ask for more information or a clearer explanation. It's up to you what you put into your body and there's little point in your GP prescribing medication for you if you're not happy with it and you won't take it.

It seems likely that some GPs are afraid to give their patients too much information about drugs and their possible side-effects – such as weight gain or blurred vision – in case they discourage the patient from taking the drug. But it's always better to know what you are facing up to, so that you can make a sensible, informed choice: so always ask to be treated like an intelligent adult.

Following recent NHS reorganization, it is now much easier to change your GP – all you have to do is find another doctor willing to take you on as a patient.

Drugs and other therapies

Most migraine sufferers find they need medication, whether only from time to time or on a regular basis. Some people rely on the occasional aspirin, whereas others have to take long-term preventative medication. Unfortunately, there is no single 'wonder-drug' which works for everyone, and some people have to try numerous combinations of drugs and other therapies before they find something that works for them. Every migraine patient is different and the treatment needs to be tailored according to their specific needs.

The encouraging fact is that everyone can be helped to some extent: there are no 'hopeless cases'. What matters is a combination of three factors:

1. Your GP's willingness to listen, advise, experiment, if necessary, and be flexible; this could mean a readiness to accept that conventional and alternative therapies can work hand-in-hand to arrive at the optimum solution to your problems;
2. Your willingness to co-operate and take an active role in your own treatment;
3. Your refusal to be satisfied with less than the best: if a drug doesn't work or has side-effects, it is your responsibility to say so and to press for an alternative strategy.

There are two main types of drug therapy:

– short-term treatment for individual attacks
– long-term (prophylactic) treatment, aimed at preventing or reducing the severity and frequency of attacks

One point to bear in mind is that any drug which is strong enough to relieve your migraine may also be strong enough to have side-effects. So it's important to obey the rules:

• Never exceed the stated dose
• Ask your doctor what to expect
• Report back to your doctor if you suffer any side-effects.

There are alternatives to most forms of medication, so the chances are that if one drug doesn't suit you, another will. So once again, don't accept less than the best. On the other hand, be realistic: don't expect a miracle cure, and be prepared for your attacks to be relieved, rather than cured altogether.

It is vital that you should follow the instructions which you are given with your medication, and also that you should take your medication at the very first sign of an attack. Your body prepares for an attack some hours before you get any physical symptoms. Systems begin to shut down, and your stomach stops working properly.

You can learn to recognize the early warning signs and respond promptly. Your doctor can prescribe an anti-sickness drug which will also improve your stomach's ability to absorb the painkillers which you take. But these will only work properly if you take them early enough. In general, soluble and effervescent (fizzy) medication is more easily absorbed than the usual tablets. It may also help if you eat something, or drink something sweet like sugary tea or lemonade, as this raises your blood-sugar level.

Drug treatments

Whereas doctors tend to be wary of prescribing drugs to young children, most adult migraine-sufferers who seek medical advice will be offered a course of drug therapy.

Whether used alone or in conjunction with other strategies such as relaxation training, drugs can help the vast majority of migraine sufferers. But, sufferers vary a great deal, so there is no single cure-all: drug therapy has to be tailored very expertly to fit the individual. You may be asked, therefore, to try a variety of different drugs, some of which will have no effect, and to persevere until at last you and your GP hit upon the right combination of drugs for you.

Obviously you will need to be patient; but you should also take an active interest in your treatment, asking questions and always expressing any worries you may have. All drugs – and that includes herbal treatments, which are often powerful drugs themselves – have side-effects, which need to be weighed up against the benefits. The eventual decision has to be yours.

Drug treatment for acute attacks

Thee are many over-the-counter painkillers which can be very helpful in treating the acute stages of a migraine attack: but remember, even over-the-counter drugs are powerful and should be treated with respect.

Research indicates that, hours before an attack begins your stomach stops working properly and becomes less able to absorb nourishment and drugs. Soluble and effervescent remedies are often the best for migraine sufferers, as they are more easily absorbed by your 'groggy' stomach. Also, your doctor can prescribe certain antisickness drugs which help the stomach to work better and reduce your feeling of nausea.

Aspirin and **paracetamol** are the two most familiar storecupboard analgesics (painkillers). It is very important that you keep to the stated dose and *never* exceed it, as an overdose can cause permanent damage. Too much paracetamol can damage the liver very seriously, while in some people aspirin can cause gastric problems. Nevertheless, used at the right time and with caution they can be very effective.

(*NB never* give aspirin to children under 16 years except on your doctor's advice.)

Caffeine is a common component of compound headache remedies like Solpadeine. It works by giving you a temporary 'lift' and shrinking the swollen blood vessels in your head. Unfortunately, caffeine is not ideal for most migraine sufferers because of the likelihood of 'rebound' headaches when the caffeine wears off and your blood vessels expand beyond their normal size, causing more pain. It may also prevent sleep, which is an important aspect of treatment. Caffeine is best used for occasional headaches, or when you need a burst of alertness, e.g. to allow you to drive home.

Ibuprofen (e.g. Nurofen) is a relative newcomer to over-the-counter sales. It was developed as an antiarthritis drug, but has proved to be an effective general painkiller. It is similar to aspirin in terms of drawbacks.

Migraleve is an over-the-counter product which may be of help in mild attacks. Tends to be very expensive.

Midrid is a combination drug sometimes very effective in treating migraine. It is available on prescription or over the counter.

Migravess is a mixture of a painkiller (aspirin) and an antisickness drug (metaclopramide) in an easily-absorbed, effervescent base. Similiar to –

Paramax (paracetamol and metaclopramide). It is a prescription-only drug. Best taken early on in an attack, for maximum effect.

Maxolon and **Domperidone** are two prescription-only anti-sickness drugs which also aid the absorption of pain killers. They are best taken early on in an attack, with pain killers, for maximum effect. They should be taken whether nausea is present or not. **Stemetil** is an anti-sickness drug only, and has no effect on gastric motility.

Ponstan is a prescription drug for headache. It is also useful for menstrual headache, as it helps the pain of periods and can reduce heavy bleeding.

Ergotamine is derived from a fungus which grows on mouldy rye. It is an effective treatment for migraine and cluster headaches, but has many drawbacks:

– it can leave patients feeling exhausted and nauseous

– an overdose or sudden withdrawal can lead to severe migraine-type headaches, so this drug is useful only in treating occasional migraines; if used regularly it can result in daily or near-daily headaches, and heart and circulation problems
– cannot be used by anyone with heart disease

Ergotamine can be prescribed as tablets, suppositories or an inhaler.

Sumatriptan is a very new drug developed by Glaxo, to treat acute attacks of migraine. It is currently undergoing clinical trials using an auto-injector. This allows patients to inject themselves with the drug as soon as they feel they need it. It will also be available on prescription, in an oral form.

Long-term (preventative) treatment

Beta-blockers (e.g. propanolol) were developed to help people with high blood pressure, but are also helpful in the treatment of anxiety and preventing attacks of migraine. A long-acting form of the drug is available (Inderal LA), which means that you simply take one, higher-dose, capsule, per day. Side-effects may include lethargy, tiredness and cold hands and feet. Asthma sufferers should not take beta-blockers, which should also not be taken with ergotamine. Patients are usually started on a very low dose taken three times a day.

Calcium antagonists are a newish addition to the armoury of antimigraine drugs, not used very often in the UK. There may be some side-effects.

Dixarit (clonidine) is still taken by many thousands of people, but recent research indicates that it may not be as useful as it was once thought to be. It is useful for menopausal symptoms, as it helps hot flushes, etc.

Sanomigran (pizotifen) is a useful drug, but can cause drowsiness, increased appetite and weight gain in some people.

Deseril (methysergide) is an effective preventive drug, but one which has fallen from favour because of its side-effects. These can sometimes be avoided by taking the drug on a five-months-on-one-month-off basis.

Anti-depressants (e.g. amitriptyline) can be helpful in preventing migraine attacks. It is thought that they have an effect on the chemical imbalance in the brain. Side-effects may include dry mouth, blurred vision, drowsiness and constipation. These side-effects are usually only present in the first two weeks of taking the drug. Beneficial effects do not occur until after this initial two-week period.

Non-steroidal anti-inflammatory drugs (NSAIDs) (e.g. aspirin; Voltarol (diclofenac sodium) were developed to combat arthritis, but are also occasionally useful in the prevention and treatment of migraine. More commonly, they are used for the acute treatment of migraine. Available in suppository form.

Prostaglandin inhibitors (e.g. ponstan (mefenamic acid)) can be used to help treat migraine attacks which are associated with menstruation.

For a list of 'alternative' over-the-counter remedies such as mineral supplements and herbal and homeopathic preparations, see p. 62.

NB: A word about suppositories! The word 'suppository' is, unfortunately, a standing joke in Britain. Our more liberated Continental cousins have been aware of the benefits of suppositories for years, and have none of our Anglo-Saxon reservations about these very useful little bullet-shaped drugs.

A suppository is an individual dose of a drug, contained in a solid waxy pellet which dissolves when it comes into contact with your body heat (which is why it's best to keep your suppositories in a cool place). All you do is insert the suppository, pointed-end first, into your rectum (back passage), pushing it up as far as it will comfortably go.

Inserting a suppository should not hurt. On the other hand, the whole process is much pleasanter if you invest in a supply of very thin, disposable plastic gloves (available from chemists, supermarkets and the Body Shop), plus a tube of lubricating jelly such as KY (your pharmacist will advise). Squatting or lying on your left side are two tried and tested positions for inserting suppositories – it needn't be a great feat of contortionism. As suppositories are greasy and tend to 'leak' a little, you may wish to protect your underwear with a pad of tissue paper.

It would be a shame if ill-founded embarrassment prevented anyone from using a form of drug therapy which is especially valuable for migraine-sufferers. Drugs are absorbed very rapidly through the wall of the rectum – much more rapidly than they would be absorbed from your stomach, especially since it stops working efficiently hours before an attack begins. So if you use suppositories, you know that the drugs you are taking will work quickly and efficiently: is that anything to feel embarrassed about?

Attending a migraine clinic

GPs cannot be experts on every single medical problem, and your doctor may feel that he or she would like you to have a second opinion from a migraine specialist.

Specialist migraine clinics are relatively few and far between, tending to be concentrated in the neurology departments of big-city hospitals. You may have to be prepared to wait a while and travel a longish distance to get an appointment – and you cannot get an appointment at a migraine clinic without first seeing your GP and obtaining a referral letter.

But in the end it is really worth it. I know from personal experience that the treatment offered in migraine clinics is second to none. It is such a tremendous relief to talk to a doctor who understands migraine and has a thorough knowledge not just of the treatments available, but of the ways in which migraine affects sufferers' lives.

At the clinic, you will be examined and questioned about your medical history, and then a treatment plan will be tailored to fit your own lifestyle, symptoms and frequency of attacks. You should expect to have to make several visits while the doctor is assessing the effects of treatment. Doctors in migraine clinics are often more imaginative about the drugs they prescribe than GPs and are more likely to know about the very latest drugs available. They are also very knowledge-able about possible side-effects. Migraine specialists will keep an eye on your progress over the months, and are quick to react if you need to change your drug therapy.

One important aspect of attending a migraine clinic is the fact that you are helping doctors to take a step nearer to finding a cure for this distressing condition: for each and every patient they treat gives them more knowledge and expertise which they can apply to their researches. In addition, public-spirited sufferers may choose to take part in one of the many clinical trials which are always running at migraine clinics. The good thing about clinical trials is that they give the ordinary sufferer a feeling of doing something useful to bring a cure a few steps nearer. If you don't wish to join a trial, do not feel that you have to. You will still be given treatment and advice.

Treatment during acute attacks

Although you will need a doctor's referral letter in order to obtain an appointment at a migraine clinic, many clinics and hospital departments operate an 'open-house' policy when it comes to treating acute attacks.

If, for example, you find yourself in the middle of London when you feel an attack coming on, you can go to one of the migraine clinics and ask for help. You will be received sympathetically, given somewhere quiet to lie down, and your migraine will be treated.

Incidentally, many migraine clinics depend on voluntary aid for their survival, so if you can help by giving a donation or taking part in a research programme, please do so.

The City of London Migraine Clinic

The City of London Migraine Clinic is a very special place. Situated in a beautiful period house in a quiet London square amid the bustle of City offices, it welcomes several thousand patients every year, from all over the world, and helps them to overcome their headaches.

Although it works in conjunction with St Bartholomew's Hospital, the Clinic is a registered charity and relies entirely on voluntary donations to keep it going. Only four of the staff are paid, and the consultants give their time free of charge. Once a year a benefit concert is held to raise funds, and the clinic's doctors even go out onto the streets to collect money on Alexandra Rose Day. Although patients aren't charged a fee, they are asked to make a donation to clinic funds.

Anyone can be seen at the clinic. All you have to do is to ask your GP to refer you. You can either ring up to make an appointment and bring the referral letter with you, or your GP can send the letter straight to the clinic and they will send you an appointment in the post.

Unlike many bustling hospital clinics, the City of London Clinic is quiet, tranquil and even cosy. Its comfortable waiting-rooms are never filled with long queues, and doctors spend around an hour with patients on their first visit to the clinic, making sure that they have been thoroughly examined and feel at ease.

In addition to the usual drug therapies, the clinic also offers a number of other special therapies, including acupuncture (at a minimal charge to cover the cost of needles). Patients are often referred to other specialists, such as orthodontic surgeons, psychotherapists or psychiatrists, if necessary and if the patient wishes to pursue those lines of treatment. Doctors will also suggest alternative therapies if they feel they would be of help. The emphasis is on treating the whole person not just the symptoms, and patients are not made to feel that they are 'guinea-pigs' for new high-tech drugs. Doctors like Anne MacGregor believe that they learn as much from their patients as their patients learn from them.

The City of London Clinic welcomes new patients, but needs money to survive: so please make a generous donation if you can.

Dentistry and why it can sometimes help

Going to the dentist may not be uppermost in your mind when you have a migraine attack, but in a limited number of cases dentistry can help.

Some sufferers have been found to have a disorder known as TMJ (tempero mandibular joint) dysfunction. In layman's terms, this means that there is some imbalance in your 'bite': your teeth don't meet together quite evenly, and this places strain on your jaw. This in turn strains the muscles and causes pain in your face – sometimes leading to migraine.

Other sufferers may get similar symptoms – not from an uneven bite, but from grinding their teeth – often at night. People who are feeling tense may unwittingly clench their teeth together, which causes tension in the facial muscles and may lead to more serious problems.

Both of these problems can sometimes be treated by your dentist, who can take an impression of your teeth and build a form of brace which you wear over them. This stops you from clenching your teeth and breaks the cycle of pain.

Dietary therapies

These days, it is fashionable to talk about food 'allergies', although strictly speaking true allergies to food are very uncommon. It is more correct to talk of 'food sensitivities' or 'food intolerance'.

A true allergic reaction takes place when the body reacts to a foreign protein as though it were an 'enemy' (like a germ), and mobilizes its defences (the white blood cells) to try to engulf and destroy it. During the 'battle' to fight off the substance, you may feel ill.

The by-products of this process are antibodies, which can be detected in a blood test. Antibodies will give the body some resistance if it encounters the same substance in the future. For example, if you have 'flu, you develop 'flu antibodies which help you to fight off the disease if you are infected again by the same 'flu strain.

This type of reaction does not generally happen with food, although it is possible to be sensitive to certain foods and environmental factors and react badly to them. There is, for example, a well-documented link between migraine and citrus fruits like oranges; and in this case the 'allergic' reaction to the food would take the form of a migraine attack.

Some food intolerances are concealed, and don't really manifest themselves properly until that food is stopped completely – at which time, withdrawal headaches can result. Occasionally, sufferers turn out to be sensitive to very common foods like wheat; and these people may actually crave the foods which make them ill. That is why some specialists suggest withdrawing favourite foods for a while.

Exclusion diets

The only universally accepted way of testing for sensitivities is called an exclusion diet. Although it is possible to carry out a modified version of this at home, it is very important that you should consult your doctor before undertaking any form of dietary therapy.

Very restrictive exclusion diets should not be adhered to for long periods without a break, as they are unlikely to provide your body with all the nutrients it needs, and can make you ill.

Although most GPs are not formally trained in clinical ecology, they do recognize the role which food sensitivities can play in causing migraine, and will probably be willing to supervise you on a limited home-based exclusion diet.

Full-scale exclusion diets

This is the approach favoured by clinical ecologists, and it is not very likely that your GP will suggest quite such a draconian programme. If you are very keen on trying it, either discuss it with your GP and ask if he or she will supervise you on the diet, write to one of the organizations listed under Useful Addresses, or ask your GP if you can be referred to a food allergy specialist.

The modified approach

If you are not very keen on the idea of such a radical approach to dietary therapy, you and your doctor can try a modified version of the diet. This involves eliminating only those foods which are known to be implicated in many people's migraine attacks, namely:

- cheese
- chocolate
- red wine
- coffee (and caffeine in general – this means tea, some fizzy drinks and even some painkillers, too)
- onions
- tomatoes
- citrus fruits, especially oranges

You would be best advised to begin by asking yourself if there are any foods which you suspect, and concentrating on these, one at a time. Don't try to eliminate all the different foods at once.

You would need to exclude a food for several weeks to be sure that any possible link had been eliminated. Sometimes attacks come on very quickly after eating a trigger food (say within half an hour), but in other cases there seems to be a 'build-up' of a certain substance in the body, so that it is only after a cumulative amount of a food has been eaten that an attack results. Hence the lengthy exclusion period.

If, after eliminating each of these foods and reintroducing them, there is no improvement in your condition, you could try eliminating wheat and milk, which cause problems for quite a few people.

Of course, not everyone is sensitive to these common culprits, and many cases of migraine have no dietary connection at all. Many more people find that other environmental triggers are at work, for example cigarette smoke, flickering light, weather changes or the smell of perfume. Others find no such connection. But it is certainly worth getting together with your doctor to investigate: there is nothing to lose and everything to gain.

More information on a self-help approach to diet and migraine is given in Chapter 7. There is a useful chapter on exclusion diets in *The Irritable Bowel Diet Book* by Rosemary Nicol, published by Sheldon Press.

A test for migraine?

Although you may be given tests to eliminate the possibility of other medical disorders, there is still no reliable test for migraine. Dr

Howard Freeman, a specialist in paediatric migraine, is very sceptical about practitioners who offer patients blood or skin testing for migraine, and concludes: 'I'm convinced it's a racket!'

Because food sensitivities do not produce antibodies, it is not really possible to check for them by means of a blood test – although some doctors and therapists have attempted to do so.

Some doctors still try to test for food sensitivities in the same way that they would use to test for an allergy to, say, grass pollen or household dust – that is, by means of a skin test. The skin on the forearm is scratched and tiny drops of a solution containing the suspected allergens are dropped onto the scratched area. After a waiting period of perhaps half an hour, the area is checked for an allergic reaction – in the form of redness and swelling.

The problem is that, like blood tests, skin sensitivity tests do not work very well for foods. In fact, there is no reliable clinical test to determine the role of foods and other environmental factors in provoking migraine tests.

These are some of the 'trendy' tests which you may be offered. Approach them with caution:

- 'RAST' test (expensive and unreliable)
- intradermal and subcutaneous provocative testing (unreliable)
- glucose tolerance test (for hypoglycaemia (low blood sugar) which can provoke attacks in some people (unreliable))

Remember, many of these tests are expensive and not very reliable. If you think foods may be the culprit, it is better to experiment by cutting out the suspect foods than to invest a lot of time and money in an unreliable test.

Doctors and other therapists who specialize in diagnosing and treating these kind of sensitivities are called clinical ecologists. Almost all of them work outside the NHS, so you would have to pay for the services of a specialist therapist. Nevertheless, it is possible to isolate food triggers yourself, under strict medical supervision.

Summing up

- Migraine should always be properly diagnosed by your doctor.
- All migraine sufferers can be helped by medical treatment.
- Specialist migraine clinics can help by tailoring treatment to suit the individual.

- A successful outcome depends on a good doctor–patient relationship, and on the patient taking an active role in his or her own treatment.
- Don't be afraid to ask questions and don't accept a form of treatment which you are unhappy with.

4

The Alternative Approach

Medical treatment in Britain tends to be very drug-oriented, and when we go to see the doctor most of us feel slightly cheated if we don't emerge clutching a prescription. Yet this isn't the picture in every Western country. Take Scandinavia, for example. There, a skilled group of physiotherapists has been trained in the use of alternative methods in treating migraine: working on the muscles of the jaw to help make them stronger and more flexible. In Britain, too, there is now a movement away from the drugs-only school of thought, and towards a broader-based approach to treatment. An increasing number of doctors, nurses and physiotherapists are taking courses in alternative specialities such as homeopathy, acupuncture, osteopathy, herbalism, hypnotism and massage. And still they cannot keep up with the growth in public demand.

Alternative medicine has seen a remarkable boom in recent years: in fact, surveys put the annual growth at something over 10% per year. So what has the world of alternative medicine to offer the migraine sufferer?

Weighing up the alternative approach

Advantages

Alternative therapies lend themselves to a totally personal approach. Most therapists are trained to deal with the whole person, not just the symptoms of an illness within that person. They are guided by the philosophy that all people are individuals, and that therefore they should all be treated individually, even if they are apparently suffering from the same disease or disorder. A good alternative therapist will spend a lot of time talking to you and devising your own personal care programme – a refreshing change.

Alternative therapies carry little risk of side-effects or complications when they are practised by qualified, professional therapists.

Most alternative therapies can be practised alongside conventional medicine, allowing the patient to take advantage of the best of both worlds. A growing number of GPs and hospital doctors are recognizing the benefits of alternative, drug-free therapies for migraine patience of all ages. In fact, more and more doctors and nurses are taking training courses in alternative therapies like homeopathy and acupuncture to complement the skills learned in their conventional medical training.

Disadvantages

It is best to have migraine diagnosed by a qualified doctor – to exclude any serious medical condition – *before* seeking treatment from alternative therapists.

Unfortunately, there is a lot of variation between therapies and therapists, and it can be a hit-and-miss business trying to find a good practitioner who is professional and with whom you can establish the right rapport. Some alternative therapies have no governing body or legal obligation to register qualified practitioners, so there is always a risk of falling into the hands of a charlatan or an incompetent practitioner.

One way to get round this problem is to attend one of the growing number of 'natural healing centres' which bring together therapists from a variety of different 'alternative' therapies, under one roof. They may also offer a formal or informal counselling service to help you select the best type of therapy for your own problem.

In rare cases, a GP may be unhappy about involvement with 'alternative' medicine, and this could lead to friction and maybe even a reluctance to refer you to a specialist migraine clinic. But stand your ground, and, if necessary, change your GP.

Alternative therapy does not, on the whole, offer instant cures, and one form of therapy which works wonders for one migraine sufferer may be totally ineffective for another. There is absolutely no way of knowing what will suit you until you have tried it. You will have to persevere for some weeks or months before you can tell if there is going to be any improvement. Needless to say, this means that you will require a lot of patience and a fair bit of cash, too.

With the exception of homeopathy and some forms of acupuncture (and osteopathy, in rare cases), so-called alternative therapies are not available under the NHS. This means that you will have to pay the therapist's full fee yourself.

As with any type of treatment – conventional medicine included – there is always the possibility of a 'placebo' effect. This happens sometimes when patients are so grateful to be offered any form of treatment that they improve for a while because they feel better psychologically, rather than because the drug or therapy itself is effective. For this reason, you need to discuss with your therapist how long to try the therapy for before you decide to continue with it or try something else: initial results could be misleading. You must also be scrupulously honest with yourself about any real or imagined improvements in your condition.

Choosing a therapist: points to watch

Since migraine is notoriously hard to treat and causes so much suffering, at any given time there will always be a large number of people who are so desperate for relief that they will spend almost any amount of time, effort and money in an attempt to find a therapy which works for them. Unfortunately, there is no general 'clearing-house' for alternative therapies, no central agency you can go to for advice on which therapy might suit you best. Likewise, there is no foolproof way of choosing a therapist. But, having chosen a therapy, there are three main points to consider as you collect information about possible practitioners, namely the therapists:

- Professional qualifications
- Reputation (particularly by word of mouth)
- Empathy.

Professional qualifications
The important questions to ask yourself are:

- what professional qualifications does the practitioner hold?
- does the practitioner belong to a nationally accredited professional body, such as the General Register of Osteopaths?

Unlike the practitioners of conventional medicine, most alternative practitioners do not have to hold recognized professional qualifications in order to practise. But clearly, you would be ill-advised to place yourself in the hands of a self-taught amateur, no matter how gifted he or she may appear to be.

Although qualifications may not be compulsory, all the major therapies now offer rigorous professional training courses and strongly advise patients only to accept treatment from trained professionals.

Registration of all alternative practitioners is not yet compulsory or universal, but it may well become so over the next few years.

Where applicable, practitioners are registered with their national professional body, and each body can supply a list of trained practitioners. A list of addresses is given at the end of this book.

The rule is: only go to a properly trained, experienced, registered professional. This way, you minimize the chances of something going wrong and maximize the chances of receiving the best possible treatment for your money. Note: just because a practitioner is qualified and registered, this does not mean that the treatment you get will be successful; no one can guarantee that, not even the NHS.

Reputation

Think: what would you do if you were moving to a new area and needed to sign on with a medical practice? The chances are that you would do some research: perhaps asking friends and neighbours to recommend general practitioners in the area.

Your research into alternative therapists should be every bit as thorough. After all, you will have to pay quite a considerable fee for the treatment you receive, and the money you spend on making your body healthier is just as much of an investment as putting your savings into the building society, shares or unit trusts!

You should be able to obtain lists of practitioners through the following outlets:

- libraries (who will also supply names and addresses of national professional bodies)
- Citizens' Advice Bureaux
- Yellow Pages

Start by asking people you know if they have had any good or bad experiences of local alternative practitioners, and weigh up the pros and cons: word of mouth is the best recommendation. When you do decide on a practitioner, it isn't a bad idea to ask if you can speak to one or more present or former patients, so that you can ask questions not only about the therapist, but about what to expect from the approach to treatment.

Remember that even within one type of therapy, there are likely to be practitioners who specialize in treating certain disorders. Within osteopathy, for example, there are a number of practitioners who specialize in treating migraine by manipulating the bones of the head (cranial osteopathy). Reputable therapists will often refer you to a colleague if they feel that he or she will be better placed to help you, or particularly interested in your type of complaint.

Don't forget to discuss the cost, too. It is worth enquiring locally about variations in consultation fees. Just because one therapist charges more or less than another, does not necessarily imply that the treatment offered is of greater or lesser quality: it could just be a question of overheads. But it is worth knowing what sort of fees you are letting yourself in for, and a fee which is substantially higher or lower than the average might prompt you to ask a few searching questions. National bodies may be able to give some guidelines on average fees charged.

Once you get face to face with your therapist, don't be afraid to talk about money, and the possible duration of treatment. It is worth asking:

- Do you think you will be able to help me?
- If so, can you estimate the length of time/number of sessions I am likely to need?
- How long will it be before I am able to see some improvement?

It may be difficult for a therapist to make confident predictions at the first meeting, but if you are attending for treatment over a period of months, with no noticeable improvement, it is time to ask yourself if you are really spending your money wisely.

Empathy

Empathy is a strange concept, but it is an important one in this context. When you place yourself (often literally) in the hands of a therapist, you are investing a great deal of trust in that person.

Some therapies, like homeopathy and hypnotherapy, involve a close examination of your feelings, motivations and personal qualities. So you may be asked some quite searching questions about yourself, and if you are uncomfortable with a therapist, this may influence the effectiveness of a treatment. Likewise, if you are undertaking a form of therapy in which muscle relaxation is an important component – say, massage, or Alexander Technique – you will not be doing yourself or your therapist any favours by being tense.

Above all, remember that you do not have to feel guilty if you simply don't like a particular practitioner: and you certainly don't have to persevere just because of some misguided sense of loyalty.

If you're not happy, move on. It's your choice. Some people like or dislike each other instantly, for no definable reason, and that's just a fact of life. Many migraine patients are lacking in assertiveness, and this can only make matters worse if it places you under unspoken stress. Shop around if need be, and don't accept less than the best.

Choosing a therapy

Because there is so much variation between therapies and therapists, it would be pointless to try to make too many sweeping statements or predictions about alternative treatments.

What I shall try and do here is give a general impression of what to expect when you visit a therapist, and the general principles of a number of well-established therapies.

Acupuncture

There are two main forms of acupuncture: the traditional Chinese form, and the type adopted by conventional Western medicine. The main difference is in the philosophy behind the technique.

Chinese acupuncture is based on the idea that the healthy body contains an essential balance between two complementary forms of energy, Yin and Yang. In the diseased body, this balance is disturbed. Traditional acupuncture aims to restore the energy balance by placing needles at certain vital energy centres in the body. Inserting the needles is said to redirect the body's energies along the correct pathways, so helping the body to heal itself.

Western medical acupuncture aims more at symptomatic relief: there is no mystical philosophy behind it. Doctors use acupuncture techniques to reduce pain and discomfort, sometimes using a gentle electric current which gives extra relief. Medical acupuncture eases pain, but does not claim to cure the underlying disorder.

If you decide to give acupuncture a try, you are most likely to encounter the Chinese system. This traditional approach is designed to treat the whole person, rather than just relieve symptoms. Scientific studies have shown that it can work, though nobody is quite sure why.

What to expect

You may find the approach taken by the acupuncturist rather strange, compared to your experience of the good old NHS 'bedside manner'. You will be asked lots of questions, some of which you may think are irrelevant, but the practitioner is trying to build up a rounded picture of you as a person. This is an important principle of Chinese medicine.

The acupuncturist may examine your tongue and spend a lot of time feeling your pulse. These are two techniques said to give a strong indication of your general physical condition. Chinese practitioners claim that they can feel as many as six distinct pulses in your wrist, and that any irregularities in them give clues as to your physical problems.

The actual process of putting the needles in is virtually painless. The needles themselves are so thin that you will hardly feel them going in, and they hardly ever draw any blood. All qualified and reputable acupuncturists are scrupulous about sterilizing their needles, so there should be no risk of infection.

There are two approaches to treating migraine. In the first, the needles are placed not in the head but in the lower arms and legs, where the relevant energy pathways are said to be. The second school of thought uses just the earlobe, which is said to carry a sort of mini-map of the body's energy pathways.

Individual treatments may last from 10 to 20 minutes, but you will probably have to have a course of several sessions.

Pros and cons

The big advantage of acupuncture is that it uses no harmful drugs and is virtually painless. Even if it doesn't cure your migraine attacks directly, you may derive some benefit just from having to lie still and relax for 20 minutes.

The only real disadvantage – apart from the cost, of course – is the fact that it certainly doesn't work for everyone. But then, as we have so often said, all migraine sufferers are different and you may just turn out to be one of the ones who are helped by acupuncture.

The City of London Migraine Clinic has its own in-house acupuncture service, which it offers to suitable patients at a minimal cost.

Self-help potential?

Obviously acupuncture does not lend itself to the self-help enthusiast. On no account should you *ever* stick needles into yourself, for whatever reason.

However, the general principles of acupuncture can be adapted for self-help through 'acupressure'. This is a technique involving exerting firm pressure on the relevant energy-centres, and particularly on points in the head, neck, wrists and hands. Details are given in Chapter 7.

Homeopathy

Homeopathy has seen a huge growth in popularity over the past few years, though it has in fact been around for a very long time. It is a system of treatment formalized by Dr Hahnemann around two hundred years ago, based on the principle that 'like treats like'.

The basic idea is that a plant or mineral extract which, in large quantities, would cause a disorder, can be effective in treating that same disorder when given in minute quantities. The substance is diluted many hundreds of times, and the quantity of the substance actually left in the solution is so small that it is actually sub-molecular.

Critics of the system say that the treatment cannot possibly be effective, because it goes against all the laws of medicine and physics. Yet independent research projects at prestigious medical centres such as Glasgow Royal Infirmary have indicated that homeopathic remedies really can work in some cases. Further controlled trials are necessary.

The success of these remedies is greater than could reasonably be attributed to a 'placebo' effect – but no one has yet been able to unravel this enigma. One theory is that the solution retains a 'memory' of the original substance, even though it has been diluted so many times that there is probably none of the drug left in it!

Whilst scientists continue to look for an explanation, homeopathic practitioners all over the world simply accept that the system can work, and are getting on with treating a huge range of disorders. There is a growing number of conventionally trained doctors who also practise homeopathy, and homeopathic treatment is sometimes obtainable under the NHS at certain hospitals in the United Kingdom.

What to expect

Consulting a homeopathic practitioner is not quite like going to see your GP (though a growing number of homeopaths *are* GPs). As well as examining you and asking you to describe your symptoms, the practitioner will ask you what may seem to be a range of irrelevant questions, such as: 'Do you prefer being warm or cool?' or 'Are you a strong-willed person?'

The reason for all this is that homeopathic treatments vary

between individuals: two people who are apparently suffering from the same illness may be offered different medicines to take. This is because homeopaths believe that they are treating the whole person, restoring the energy balance so that the body can heal itself. They are not just prescribing drugs to treat the symptoms.

Don't be surprised or disappointed if you go away with only one or two little pills to take: homeopathy is not like taking a 7-day course of antibiotics. But it is important that you take the medication exactly as specified, even if you are tempted to think: 'How on earth could that tiny thing have any effect?'. The fact is that homeopathic remedies do seem to have produced some amazing successes, however unlikely it may seem.

Occasionally, a homeopath may take the view that homeopathic and conventional medicine cannot be taken simultaneously. If you are taking any prescription drugs for your migraine, you *must* talk to your doctor before deciding to stop taking them. Some long-term preventive drugs, like beta-blockers, can cause serious problems if you stop taking them suddenly, without medical supervision.

Pros and cons

Homeopathy has certainly been found helpful by some migraine patients, though by no means all. It may be a question of persevering for quite a long time before relief is obtained, though in some cases, there may be a startling 'overnight recovery'. However, some people find that they actually feel worse before they feel better.

If you can find an NHS doctor who is also a homeopath, or if your GP will refer you to a homeopathic hospital, you may be able to receive treatment on the NHS.

Self-help potential

Homeopathic remedies are big business: you can buy them in any health-food shop and many chemists. The main problem is in knowing which one to choose, and how to administer it. Bearing in mind the care which homeopathic practitioners take to fit the remedy to the sufferer, it is hardly surprising that self-help homeopathy can be a hit-and-miss business.

For most sufferers, it is better to seek professional homeopathic help so that a remedy can be designed specifically for you, rather than to spend a lot of money on over-the-counter remedies which may simply leave you out of pocket and disillusioned with the whole business.

Nevertheless, there are some types of headache which respond to these remedies: your health-food shop will probably have a leaflet to help you decide which is best for you. A list of common remedies is given in Chapter 7.

Medical herbalism

Medical herbalism – or phytotherapy – is practised mainly by lay practitioners. If you want to give it a try, look for someone who has trained at the School of Phytotherapy in Tunbridge Wells. The qualification to look for is MIMH.

As in homeopathy, medical herbalism relies heavily on plant-based remedies. In fact, many conventional prescription drugs – like the heart drug digitalis – are also made from plants; so herbalism is not really such a revolutionary idea.

What to expect

Like any good alternative therapist, the medical herbalist lays great store by personal attention and getting to know the patient thoroughly. You will be given a thorough examination, and asked lots of questions about your medical history.

Most herbalists make up their own medicines, to order, and dispense them on the premises.

Pros and cons

You should always consult your doctor first, and tell the herbalist if you are taking any drugs. Plant remedies are also powerful drugs, and the combination might be harmful rather than helpful. It's worth remembering that herbal remedies, too, may sometimes have unpleasant side-effects.

Plant remedies certainly can help in migraine cases. Many migraine sufferers have already discovered the benefits of feverfew: trials suggest it can be helpful in around 70% of cases, though it can cause mouth ulcers and gastric irritation. The effect of its long-term use are not known. It should not be taken during pregnancy. Medical herbalism may also be able to help with other 'natural' remedies.

Self-help potential

Feverfew can be grown in your own garden or bought in tablet or capsule form from health-food shops. More details about this interesting and useful herb are given in Chapter 7.

Osteopathy and chiropractic

It may seem odd that manipulating bones can improve migraine symptoms, but it has proved effective in a number of cases, particularly where there is some sort of skeletal imbalance.

To the lay person, osteopathy and chiropractic seem very similar, since they both involve manipulation. In fact, they arise from rather different philosophies and chiropractic tends to specialize in trapped nerves (not usually a factor in migraine).

Osteopaths, like chiropractors, do a lot of work with the spine; but they also manipulate other bones, with the aim of correcting any misalignment and so helping the body to rediscover its natural poise and balance, free from unnatural stresses and strains.

Some osteopaths have branched out into a specialism called cranial osteopathy. This is a treatment specifically designed for migraine and tension headaches. The idea is that the skilled osteopath is able to move the bones of the skull a minute amount, and this is supposed to help improve blood flow and ease muscle tension. However, this remains a controversial therapy as conventional doctors claim it is impossible to move the bones of the skull after thay have become knit together in early childhood.

What to expect

There are far too many horror stories and music-hall jokes about osteopaths. The common perception of a sadistic muscle-man, wrenching arms and legs out of their sockets, is very far from the truth!

Osteopaths are highly skilled practitioners of a subtle and often very gentle art. Remarkably little discomfort is involved, and patients sometimes report dramatic improvements, particularly with back pain and sports injuries.

Migraine may not be treated simply with cranial massage. The osteopath will be examining you closely for signs such as poor posture, stiff neck and shoulder muscles, bad spinal alignments etc, as any spinal imbalance throws the whole body off balance, placing unnatural stresses and strains upon it. This in turn causes muscle tension, which is a factor in many cases of both tension headache and migraine. So treatment may involve manipulation of the back, neck and shoulders.

Pros and cons

It is very important to seek out a qualified, reputable practitioner:

lists of registered osteopaths can be obtained from the General Register, or you can look for registered practitioners in the Yellow Pages.

Doctors used to be very wary of osteopaths, tending to think that they could actually make problems worse rather than better. These days, they take a much more open-minded approach, and an increasing number of GPs now refer cases – e.g. for intractable back pain – to recommended local osteopaths.

Osteopathic treatment of migraine is a less thoroughly tried and tested therapy, but it can have spectacular results for a few people. We are not always aware of our bad posture or other skeletal problems which can manifest themselves or certainly contribute to head pain.

If you're thinking of consulting an osteopath, it's extremely advisable to consult your doctor first; in any case, your GP may be able to recommend a practitioner to you. Osteopathy is occasionally available on the NHS.

Self-help potential

Not under any circumstances. Though a gentle scalp massage can be soothing.

Alexander Technique

The Alexander Technique is not so much a medical therapy, as a way of life. It is used extensively by actors, singers and dancers to improve their breathing and posture, and it can help anyone to achieve a greater sense of physical wellbeing.

The system was devised by F. Matthias Alexander, who was born in Australia in 1869 and died in 1955. As a child he was a semi-invalid, but the techniques which he developed helped him to restore his own health. He then set about teaching his system to other people.

Alexander discovered that efficient use of the body depends on a proper relationship of the head, neck and back. The head should be delicately balanced on top of the spinal column by small muscles. When the larger outside muscles of the neck take over, they contract the spine and produce tensions throughout the body. The Alexander Technique aims to eliminate these tensions, promoting body awareness and better 'use of the self'.

What to expect

A skilled instructor (who has taken a three-year course of training) will guide you through the technique: the Society of Teachers of the Alexander Technique can supply a list of properly qualified teachers. Individuals vary, but on average you will need around 25 lessons.

Teaching is an active process: the instructor touches and guides you gently, to stimulate your own body-awareness.

The Alexander Technique improves posture, and should promote general physical wellbeing as well as alleviating your migraine if there is a postural factor in your attacks.

Self-help potential

The Alexander Technique cannot be self-taught: you *must* be guided by a skilled instructor. But, once you have learned the basics, you are equipped – and expected – to continue to make progress on your own. Success depends very much upon a positive contribution from yourself, and on a good two-way relationship between pupil and teacher, not just a passive acceptance of what the teacher says or does to you.

Massage, reflexology and aromatherapy

Massage therapies have gained in popularity over the last few years, and there is no doubt at all that gentle massage can be very effective in reducing muscle tensions.

Trigger-point therapy is a type of intensive massage aimed at breaking the vicious circle of tension. A trigger-point is a little, tender spot – usually on the head, neck, shoulders or upper back – which marks the place where a muscle has gone into a state of chronic tension, a spasm. This tender spot is a sort of nucleus of pain and tension, which remains there permanently and triggers off more generalized tension from time to time, often leading to head and neck pain.

A trigger-point is very painful to the touch, and when you press it you may feel the pain some distance away: for example, you touch a spot on your shoulder, but feel the pain in your hand.

What to expect

Trigger-point therapists apply firm pressure to each trigger-point in turn, until each one is 'deactivated' and the cycle is broken. The technique can also be taught to one of your friends, so that he or she can repeat the treatment as necessary.

Self-help potential

Trigger-point massage of the head and neck, and of corresponding acupressure points on the hands, can be easily learned and self-administered.

Hypnotherapy

There may be a stress factor in your migraine, in which case not only relaxation but also hypnotherapy and psychotherapy may be of some help.

It is important to understand that hypnosis is not something which is inflicted upon a patient. You cannot be hypnotized if you do not want to be, and your mind cannot be 'taken over'. Hypnosis is like a very deep form of relaxation – close to the mental state you are in just before you fall asleep – and you can break out of it at any time you choose.

Once you are in a state of hypnosis, you become more responsive to suggestions. This can help you to overcome stress, or isolate the other factors which trigger off your migraine attacks.

Some hypnotherapists will teach you how to induce this state in yourself, to help you relax more deeply. Recent hospital trials involving migraine patients have had some success.

An increasing number of GPs have been trained in hypnosis, and the British Society of Medical and Dental Hypnosis will advise.

Psychotherapy

Psychotherapy is a one-to-one technique aimed at discovering deep-seated problems, bringing them to the surface and helping you to devise strategies to come to terms with them. For example, you may have a problem in asserting yourself because you have a low self-image. This can lead to a feeling of enormous stress, which of course is an important trigger factor in migraine.

Psychotherapy is often a gruelling process, demanding considerable commitment from the subject as well as the therapist. Trust is essential, which is why you must only consult a reputable, thoroughly-trained professional. Your GP may be able to recommend a therapist, and there are some subsidized schemes under the NHS.

Clinical ecology

The principle behind exclusion diets is that you eliminate from your diet all the foods and liquids which you suspect may be causing your disease – in this case, migraine. In order to do this, it is usual to follow a very basic 'Stone Age' diet for several days, to eliminate all traces of 'suspect' foods from the body.

The foods which are considered *least* likely to cause adverse reactions are:

- lamb
- pears
- courgettes
- carrots
- runner and French beans
- rice
- bottled spring water.

All foods should be organically produced if possible, to reduce the possibility of contamination by pesticides, etc.

If this seems like a very restricted list, it is worth bearing in mind that many of the worst culprits are everyday foods like milk and wheat, which are a part of many common dishes, so these have to be eliminated early on.

After five days on this diet, you begin to introduce extra foods one at a time, noting down any adverse reactions. If you suffer a migraine attack after eating a particular food or additive, then you know that you are probably sensitive to it and that you should eliminate it from your diet.

It is worth noting that clinical ecologists believe that trigger foods are often favourite foods, the ones you eat frequently. If you stop eating them, you may get withdrawal symptoms such as 'rebound' headaches: so you might well feel worse before you feel better. Fasting can also give you a headache because of low blood-sugar levels.

Never begin any form of exclusion diet without first consulting your doctor and having a thorough medical check-up. Your doctor may also be able to supervise you on the diet, or recommend a reputable alternative therapist.

Over-the-counter 'alternative' remedies

Feverfew (*Tanacetum parthenium*) is a member of the daisy family, and is a common herb which you can grow in your own garden. If you want to grow your own feverfew, it is very important that you obtain the right plant, so ask at your local nursery.

In a recent trial at the City of London Migraine Clinic, 70% of sufferers reported an improvement in their migraines after taking feverfew. A trial at Nottingham University Hospital also produced encouraging results.

Leaves can be taken fresh or dried – about two or three small leaves per day is a normal preventive dose. It tastes rather bitter, so some people like to take it in a sandwich. Alternatively, you can obtain feverfew in capsule or tablet form from your local chemist or health-food shop.

Points to remember:

- it may take up to six weeks of daily medication before any effect is noticed
- some people get mouth ulcers and gastric upsets from taking feverfew
- tablets offer feverfew in a controlled dose
- it should not be taken when pregnant or breast feeding
- the effects of long-term use are not known

DLPA and calcium D-phenylalanine is an amino acid which helps the body's natural pain-killers to work better, so it is said to be good for anyone who suffers from constant pain.

Calcium gluconate, taken daily with vitamin D, is thought to have an effect in reducing pain.

Both of these products are available from health-food stores. Be careful to follow the instructions on the bottle, and never take any remedy – however seemingly innocent and 'natural' it may be – without consulting your doctor first.

Homeopathic remedies

Because homeopaths tailor their remedies to suit the individual patient and his or her personality, as well as the symptoms, there is no single homeopathic remedy for headaches.

If you want to try taking over-the-counter homeopathic preparations, it is best to obtain a leaflet (often available in health-food shops) and read up on the subject before you buy. Homeopathic preparations come in various dilutions, the most popular of which are called 12C and 6C. They come in tablet form, and should be dissolved in the mouth slowly.

There are two main types of homeopathic treatments: preventive preparations and tablets to take during an attack.

Preventive treatments (also used for chronic headaches)

Natrum muriaticum may be used for the prevention of migraine. It is also suitable for nervous people with watery eyes and greasy, spotty skins.

Kali bichromicum may be used for people with sinus problems and catarrh, and for headaches which are made worse by stooping.

Cimifuga may be taken for headaches which begin at the back of the head and are associated with aching neck muscles. Also for pre-menstrual headaches.

Silica may be taken for headaches which begin at the back of the head and rise up to cover the top of the head. They may also be on the right side of the head, and may be made worse by noise and draughts.

Sepia may be taken for headaches which improve with sleep or violent exertion, and headaches associated with nausea.

Lachesis may be taken for menopausal headaches which are better in a cold atmosphere.

Treatment during attacks

Glonoine is used for headaches associated with too much sun, and for pounding headaches.

Bryonia is indicated for sufferers with dark hair and skin. Headaches are worse on movement but may be relieved by pressure.

Spigelia may be taken for headaches on the left side, before or after a period.

Iris versicolor is indicated for acute migraine attacks with nausea or vomiting, and 'weekend' headaches.

Gelsemium may be taken for 'flu-type headaches and muscle tension.

China sulph is indicated for headaches which start at the back of the head, then spread. The patient is nauseous but wants to eat, and may feel worse in the open air or on turning the head or eyes.

Sanguinaria may be taken for premenstrual headaches, on the right side, with dizziness and nausea. Also for headaches caused by too much sun.

Summing up

- Always check with your doctor before you embark on any alternative therapy: a complete check-up will ensure that other medical conditions are not present.
- An increasing number of GPs are becoming involved in alternative therapies.
- Alternative and conventional treatments can sometimes be used to complement each other.
- The main advantage with drug-free approaches is that they are less likely to result in unpleasant side-effects.
- Always make sure that you find a therapist who is fully-qualified and experienced. If possible, ask other people for their personal recommendations. Talk to the therapist before you commit yourself to a course of treatment.

5

When Is a Migraine
Not a Migraine?

When is a migraine attack not a migraine attack? Simple: when it's one of the millions of other headaches which people suffer from all over the world, every day of the year. If you suffer from headaches, migraine is not the most likely cause of them: in statistical terms only around 10% of the British population are migraine sufferers.

Headaches are an almost universal problem. Perhaps as few as 1% of people claim never to suffer from them, whilst millions of British men and women suffer from regular, severe head pain. A recent survey undertaken in America revealed that 90% of males and 95% of females reported one or more headaches in the previous 12 months, whilst 8% of males and 14% of females had missed at least one day's work or schooling through headaches during the same period.

Oddly enough, most headache sufferers still do not seek medical advice. It is thought that perhaps only 50% of migraine sufferers have ever discussed this with a doctor, and only 20% have seen a doctor in the previous year. Interestingly, about 30% of patients who have consulted a doctor about their migraine never go back.

Yet headaches are of massive economic significance worldwide. Statistics issued by the National Headache Foundation of America suggest that headaches cripple more Americans than motorcycle accidents, car collisions and industrial accidents put together.

However, headache is also a symptom in over 50 different medical conditions. Anyone who suffers from persistent, regular or severe headaches, or headaches which suddenly change in character or severity, should consult a doctor *immediately*. Self-help may be a good idea, but self-diagnosis definitely isn't: far better to be safe than sorry.

Types of non-migraine headache

There are various different types of non-migraine headache which often have to be discounted before a positive diagnosis of migraine can be made. Even if you have already been diagnosed as suffering from migraine, it is worth knowing about other types of headache.

The world of the headache is a complex one, and it is quite common to suffer from more than one type of headache pain either simultaneously (combined headache), or at different times (mixed headaches). Thus, a migraine sufferer may also suffer from tension headaches, which may be the cause or the result of the migraine attacks. Sometimes the cycle is so well-established that it is difficult to decide where one headache stops and the next one begins.

Tension headache

Around 88% of all headaches are classified as 'tension headaches'. This name is, in fact, very misleading, and it would be much more accurate to describe them as 'muscle contraction headaches'. The pain is caused by sustained contraction of the muscles in the face, neck, shoulders and/or jaw, which in turn affects the nerves in the head and causes pain.

If the muscle contraction continues for a long period of time, changes may occur in the physical structure of the muscles: they may become fibrous and inelastic, whereas normally they would be flexible and soft. As a result, the pain can become chronic and jeopardize the quality of the sufferer's life. The pain is usually described by sufferers as dull or steady, and the expression 'like a helmet' is often used. Pain is often felt on both sides of the head and may occur daily, though headaches can sometimes be one-sided and confused with migraine attacks.

There are really two distinct types of muscle contraction headache: acute and chronic. Acute attacks are usually triggered by stress or anxiety, and respond to over-the-counter drugs, relaxation and the withdrawal of the original stress factor. Chronic tension headaches are harder to treat. Some people have daily, or even continuous, headaches – though the pain may vary in intensity at different times of the day. These headaches often do not respond to ordinary painkillers, and other forms of treatment have to be considered.

Learning relaxation or biofeedback techniques may help, and antidepressants have been shown to be useful, even in patients who are not clinically depressed. Beta-blockers – which may also be used in the long-term treatment of migraine – are sometimes used when the patient is anxious.

So-called 'mixed' headaches are very common in people who suffer from regular head pain. This may mean separate attacks of tension headache and migraine, or combined attacks in which a tension headache develops into a migraine attack or (more rarely) a migraine attack turns into a tension headache.

The causes of tension headache are many and varied, but include the following:

- The stresses and strains of daily life (which may cause clenching of the jaw-muscles, grinding of the teeth etc). A busy life may also mean a poor diet, missed meals and so on, which can lead to problems with low blood sugar and headaches. But it is important to understand that muscle tension and nervous tension are not one and the same thing: and sufferers from tension headaches may be no more 'tense' than other people who never suffer from headaches.
- Emotional and psychological factors, e.g. nervous tension, depression, fear, anxiety. Suppressed emotions can be particularly destructive. For example, if you are feeling great anger or resentment towards someone but do not feel capable of expressing your feelings openly, your body will find another way of externalizing those feelings, perhaps through muscle contraction which in turn leads to headache pain.
- Posture and mechanical factors. Many of the activities of modern life are bad for the body's natural posture, though we may not realize that we are holding our bodies awkwardly and the only outward sign may be pain – say, in the shoulders, back, neck or head. Although an increasing number of office designers now take ergonomics seriously, there are still many badly designed office chairs, desks, VDUs etc, all of which can cause postural problems which may need attention from a physiotherapist or osteopath. On the home front, it is well worth checking out any activities like telephoning, sewing, watching TV, reading and simply sitting, which may encourage bad posture.

Analgesic headaches

One major problem with tension headache is that many sufferers obtain little or no relief with pain-killing drugs like aspirin or paracetamol, and there is always a danger that they will take more and more of these drugs in the hope that a bigger dose will have a greater effect.

Over-the-counter drugs may appear harmless, but all drugs are powerful and have side-effects, and any overdose could cause permanent damage to the body. Aspirin can cause peptic ulcers in people with sensitive stomachs, and a paracetamol overdose can be lethal.

What's more, recent research suggests that people who take regular, very moderate doses of analgesics every week may actually make their headaches worse, not better. The same applies to migraine drugs like ergotamine, as Dr Anne MacGregor explains: 'If you don't take the drug early enough, and if you accidentally take too much of it, a lot of the side-effects are very similar to the symptoms that you get in a migraine attack.' So moderation is the watchword in any drug-based approach to treatment.

If at all possible, drugs should be avoided as preventative treatments in favour of non-drug therapies like relaxation and lifestyle management, since drugs only treat the symptoms – not the underlying cause.

Case study Jeremy was a computer programmer. His job involved sitting at a VDU for hours on end, and as his boss was very demanding he often found himself working late and snacking or missing out meals altogether in order to meet increasingly impossible deadlines.

His home life was happy, but hectic: his wife had just had a baby, and they already had two small children under five. A large mortgage meant that money was always tight and this in turn meant that Jeremy felt he had to work harder and aim for promotion.

Jeremy found that he had an almost permanent headache which got gradually worse as the day went on, especially on those days when he spent a long time at the computer screen. He noticed that the muscles in his shoulders, neck and the back of his head felt taut and painful to the touch.

Having a permanent headache made him grumpy and worried, and he kept himself going with frequent cups of strong coffee which seemed to perk him up for a little while. Pain-killers did not seem to have much effect, and he tended to exceed the dose on the packet, in the hope that a bigger dose would being him more relief.

Jeremy's headaches were caused by a combination of factors:

- nervous tension, leading to the production of high levels of adrenaline and other 'stress chemicals'. These chemicals are designed to prepare the body for a 'flight or fight' response to dangerous situations. One of the effects of this is to increase muscle tension.

- too much caffeine from all those cups of coffee, leading to more muscle tension.
- bad posture: his chair and computer screen were badly designed and he tended to slouch, putting excessive strain on his shoulder and neck muscles.
- regular use of analgesics.

Cluster headache

Cluster headache used to be classified along with migraine, but is now recognized as a separate disorder. It is a rare but very distressing affliction, affecting men mainly and particularly men who smoke or who have smoked in the past.

Attacks come in 'clusters' lasting 6–12 weeks, and may recur at the same time every year. In a small proportion of sufferers (around 20%) the headaches may become chronic and be present all year round, making them especially distressing and difficult to treat. Each attack is short (lasting from 30 minutes to 2 hours) and there may be several attacks in any one 24-hour period, often waking the sufferer in the middle of the night. Some sufferers can predict them so accurately that they have been called 'alarm-clock headaches'.

The pain is one-sided and excruciating – like a knife in the side of the head. On the affected side, the eye waters and turns red and the eyelid droops, and there may also be stuffiness or a runny nostril. The other side is usually normal. So dreadful is the pain that the sufferer will usually not be able to sit or lie still, and may pace the room. Some sufferers pound the walls with their fists, or even bang their heads against the wall in their distress.

Unlike migraine, cluster headache has no hereditary component, and is also not thought to be stress-related: attacks often occur when the sufferer is at his or her most relaxed (e.g. during sleep).

During a 'cluster' period, it seems that the sufferer's blood vessels change in some way which makes them especially sensitive to certain influences: smoking, alcohol, histamine or nitroglycerine tablets (prescribed for angina sufferers) can all trigger off attacks at these times, even if the patient is not usually sensitive to these substances outside the cluster periods.

Nowadays, the pain of cluster headache can be helped greatly by the right medication, such as ergotamine, which constricts the blood vessels. Oxygen inhalation has also been found to be useful during attacks.

Case study Jennie was not a typical cluster headache sufferer. She was a busy young wife and mother, not an overweight middle-aged man; neither did she smoke. But every six months or so, she would suffer an agonizing bout of cluster headaches, sometimes as many as six or seven in one day. As one attack was ending, another was beginning.

Some attacks were so severe that she banged her head against the wardrobe door, because somehow that type of pain seemed less severe. Her family could not understand how anyone could be in so much pain with 'just a headache', and this made life even more difficult for her to bear.

This went on for several years, until finally Jennie was at the end of her tether and so ill that she was afraid to go out. But the story has a happy ending. After consulting a sympathetic GP, Jennie attended a migraine clinic. Within a few days she was taken into hospital; and after her condition had been stabilized, it was successfully treated with drug therapy. She is now busy and confident, and describes the change in her life as 'miraculous'.

Causes of other non-migraine headaches

Chinese Restaurant syndrome

One characteristic of Chinese restaurants is that they often add large amounts of monosodium glutamate to the food, which has a strong effect on the blood vessels of the head and can cause a very unpleasant headache. Some migraine sufferers also find that this additive can provoke an attack.

Usually, a monosodium glutamate headache comes on about half an hour after eating a Chinese meal with a lot of added msg, and lasts for about an hour. There is pain in the forehead and a throbbing sensation in the temples. Some people find that they are only affected if they consume monosodium glutamate on an empty stomach – so this is one strategy to try if you are a Chinese food addict!

A word of warning: monosodium glutamate doesn't only surface in Chinese food. It is used as a flavour enhancer by just about every manufacturer of processed foods, so if you know you are sensitive to this chemical it is a good idea to check the labels of everything you buy – or, better still, eat only fresh foods!

Processed meats

This is very similar to Chinese Restaurant Syndrome, in that it is caused by a chemical present in food. In this case, it is caused by the nitrites and nitrates used to colour processed meats, and which can produce a throbbing headache in those who are sensitive to them.

Nitrites and nitrates are found in a variety of processed meats, including hot dogs, salami and bacon. Check the labels on the packets or ask the assistant in the delicatessen.

Ice-cold food

Some people find that eating very cold food – e.g. ice cream or sorbets – gives them sudden, brief but severe headaches. Other people get severe toothache. Sadly, the only cure is to avoid the foods.

Hangovers

Hangovers happen because the blood vessels in the head are dilated (expanded) by the action of the alcohol we drink. As in migraine headaches, it is the expansion of the blood vessels which causes the pain.

As yet, there is no foolproof way to avoid hangovers, though drinking a lot of milk or water – or, after drinking, fruit juice and paracetamol (effervescent) – may help. The worst offenders in the hangover stakes are red wine, cider, whisky and brandy because of the additives or congeners they contain.

Eye problems

Contrary to popular belief, it's not all that common for a headache to be caused by eye-strain, though it's always a good idea to visit your optician if you have any problems with or worries about your eyes.

To avoid straining your eyes, read in a good light and if possible angle your book using a lectern or reading stand. Watching television in a darkened room also gives many people headaches, and can trigger off attacks in some migraine sufferers.

One very serious eye problem which includes headache symptoms is glaucoma. In glaucoma, there is a dangerous rise in pressure inside the eyeball. This causes severe pain and blurred vision, and unless treated promptly it may lead to blindness. This disease is often passed on in families, and if you have a relative who suffers from glaucoma you are entitled to a free sight test under the NHS. So if you have any worries at all, go and see your optician now.

Temporal arteritis

This is quite a rare disease which affects mainly the over-50s, but occasionally sufferers may be younger. It involves the inflammation of one of the arteries in the head. The area over the artery will be tender to touch and may be red, and there may also be visual problems. If caught in time, this disease is easily treated with steroids; but if left untreated, it can cause serious eye problems and even blindness. Your GP can carry out a simple blood test to set your mind at rest.

Brain tumours

Many, many headache sufferers worry that they may have a brain tumour, especially if a family member or friend has suffered from this disorder. Yet brain tumours are *very* rare indeed, and produce a variety of symptoms, only one of which is headache. Discuss your fears and ask if you need to have any tests. After all, suppressing your worries can only make your headaches worse.

If you have *constant* headache accompanied by symptoms like slurred speech, memory problems, loss of balance or severe vomiting, it is essential that you contact your doctor immediately.

Spinal problems

If tension headaches can be caused by habitually poor posture, leading to muscle tension, it is hardly surprising that spinal problems can have the same effect.

Every year, osteopaths and chiropractors see thousands of people whose headaches are either caused or made worse by imbalances in the alignment of the bones of the back, neck or skull. Some doctors are still sceptical abut this, but it stands to reason that if you are holding yourself in an unnatural position – for whatever reason – you are putting a strain on your muscles and this may lead to pain.

Gentle exercise is good for improving body-awareness and flexibility, and a system of neck exercises devised by Dr Mackenzie is very good for anyone with a stiff or weak neck. The Alexander Technique also promotes better posture.

Dental problems

In recent years, much publicity has surrounded the role which dental abnormalities can play in causing headaches and migraine. A few dentists even suggested that the small amounts of mercury used in dental fillings might be responsible for headache pain, and advocated replacing all fillings with non-mercury based alternatives. So far, the arguments in favour of this rather radical (and very expensive) approach have not been totally convincing.

On the other hand, it is definitely true that the misalignment of a jaw or grinding of teeth can strain the facial muscles, which in turn may lead to headaches and exacerbate migraine attacks. More details of corrective dental treatment are given in Chapter 3 (see p. 43).

High blood pressure

High blood pressure or hypertension is a serious medical problem and you *must* consult your GP if you think you may be suffering from it. Headaches may be a symptom, but on no account should you attempt self-diagnosis. If in doubt, check it out.

Injury

Any headache which follows *any* head or neck injury – especially in children – should be regarded with suspicion, and referred immediately to your doctor or the Accident and Emergency department of your local hospital.

A few people find that an injury (e.g. following car accident) triggers off a very first migraine attack, after which time they may become lifelong migraine sufferers, though many people may never have another attack.

Infections

Infections are a relatively rare cause of headache pain, though worth bearing in mind. Ear infections are quite common in children, and can often be treated quickly and effectively with antibiotics or a simple operation.

Dental abcesses can lead to ascending infections if not treated promptly.

If you have a headache combined with a temperature, stiff neck and dislike of light, seek medical advice immediately.

Sinusitis and catarrh

We all get that awful stuffed-up feeling from time to time, when we are in the middle of a heavy head-cold. Sometimes the stuffiness results from blocked sinuses – the air holes in the front of the skull become filled with catarrhal fluid which is too thick to drain away. The pressure (sometimes combined with an infection) can lead to facial pain and headaches.

Antibiotics and decongestants can be prescribed by your doctor, or you could try simple steam inhalation. In rare cases, a small operation can be performed to drain the fluid from the sinuses.

Sexual excitement

Not the legendary bedtime excuse, but a genuine medical complaint. Benign orgasmic cephalgia is a condition which affects mostly males, causing them to have a violent headache just at the point of orgasm. Fortunately, although it is unpleasant, it is very uncommon and not harmful.

Hormonal changes

Hormonal changes in women are often implicated in migraine, and can also cause other types of headache. Many women find they get headaches around the time of their periods, and some also feel vulnerable around the time of ovulation (mid-cycle). Taking the oral contraceptive pill or HRT also causes headaches in some women.

Migraine

Migraine is the biggest single cause of regular headache pain, after tension headache. It may affect as many as 10 million people in the UK alone, and it accounts for much suffering and many millions of working days lost each year. When you put that together with all the other types of headaches we have looked at, collectively they account for an awful lot of pain and suffering – much of which is avoidable or amenable to treatment.

Summing up

- There are many types of non-migraine headache, and it is quite common to suffer from both migraine and non-migraine headaches.
- Tension (muscle contraction) headache is much more common than migraine.
- Any persistent or severe headache should be reported to your doctor and investigated.

6

The Home Front: Giving Practical and Emotional Support

If you live with, or care about, someone who suffers from migraine, you have set yourself a hard task. In fact, in some ways it is more difficult to live with a migraine sufferer than it is to suffer from the migraine yourself.

The migraine sufferer knows his own beast: knows what sets it snarling, what irritates it, what pacifies it until at last it slopes back into its cage, to lurk there until the next time. The friend, relative or lover can only look on in horror, anguish or bewilderment, not understanding what is happening to this person whom they love, and not having the first idea of what to do about it.

In Chapter 1, we looked at the effects which migraine has on the daily lives of sufferers, and some of the feelings which they experience. Friends and relatives may find it helpful to read that chapter – as well as this one – as it is designed to provide an insight into the world of migraine, for non-sufferers.

The 'chocolate teapot' syndrome

I talked to many friends and relatives of migraine sufferers when I was researching my book. 'How do you feel when your friend is having an attack?', I asked. 'Helpless', they replied. 'About as much use as a chocolate teapot.'

The 'chocolate teapot' syndrome is a familiar one to anyone who has ever witnessed someone's sufferings and been unable to do anything to alleviate them. It is like that awful moment when you witness a road accident and desperately want to help . . .

But it really is important for you to get involved: to learn to understand both your own feelings and those of your friend or partner. Ironically, one common trigger of migraine is the fear of an attack – a fear which is added to every time the sufferer is ill, feels helpless and useless and under attack from people who appear callous or uncomprehending. If you can learn more about migraine and develop a more positive and open attitude to it yourself, then you can also reduce the pressure on the migraineur – hopefully leading in turn to a reduction in fear and (ultimately) less frequent attacks.

Case study Jean lives in York, and has found self-employment to be a satisfactory solution to her migraine problem: her hours are flexible, and can be slotted in to accommodate her attacks. But her relationships with other people are not without their problems, as she explains:

> At the back of my mind, there is always the dread that some really enjoyable event will be wrecked. I feel like a wet blanket. Some people think it's just an excuse – that I'm pleading a headache to get out of something. I also have difficulties with some people who want to fuss. I just want to be left alone. My mother-in-law particularly used to want to look after me and even when I went to bed, she would call up every 10 minutes to see if I was all right. I think after 25 years she has finally got the message!

Emotional reactions to migraine

Because you feel helpless, you may also experience a whole host of other, apparently negative emotions; for example:

- guilt
- anger
- resentment
- fear
- impatience
- indifference

Indifference

It may seem odd to say that someone who cares for a sufferer very deeply should feel indifference towards that person when he or she is suffering most acutely. And yet it is not so strange.

If you feel something very deeply, but cannot do anything to make things better, your brain has to activate some sort of defence mechanism to stop you going mad. And so you may feel numb and strangely apathetic. If you could do something positive, you would probably feel quite different.

Fear

The symptoms of migraine can sometimes be alarming, especially when you see them for the first time, or do not understand what they mean. The sufferer is obviously distressed and in pain – and if this is a first attack, he or she may not realize what is happening any more than you do.

One way to cope is to find out what you are dealing with. Once the migraine has been diagnosed, and other (more sinister) conditions eliminated, your fear should subside, particularly if an effective treatment is prescribed.

And once you have conquered your own fears and apprehensions, you can set about helping your friend to achieve a calmer state of mind, which will in turn help to ease the pain and shorten the attack.

Anger, resentment and impatience

It is hardly surprising that you sometimes have very negative feelings towards a sufferer, even if that person is someone you love very much. Quite apart from all the pain involved, migraine is a huge inconvenience – not just for the sufferer but also for his or her family and friends. If the attacks are severe and frequent, you may find yourself constantly having to cancel joint social arrangements at the last minute: and it's hard not to feel, almost subconsciously, that the friend is doing it deliberately, or being antisocial.

Migraine is a pain in both senses of the word: but if you create an atmosphere of mounting tension and resentment, you will probably make things worse. It is bad enough for the sufferer, wondering and wondering if an attack is going to come along and ruin everything again, without having to live with someone who is constantly saying 'You're not going to be ill again, are you?', or 'I suppose there's no point in making any arrangements: we'll only have to cancel them.'

If you feel angry, talk your anger through with the sufferer – don't repress it so that it poisons your relationship. But on the other hand, make a real effort to understand the sufferer's point of view: if you can take a flexible, fairly laid-back approach, there is every chance that your support and encouragement will have a positive impact on not only the migraine attacks, but also the sufferer's attitude to risk-taking, adventures and life in general.

Sometimes sufferers need their friends and families to help them help themselves. Take the case of the woman who didn't realize how many headaches she had until her children started making remarks about her constantly having headaches. She needed the jolt to give her the impetus to go along to her doctor and get her migraines sorted out.

Guilt

Of course, the natural outgrowth of these negative emotions is another negative emotion: guilt. 'Oh no, I'm doing it again', you groan, as you realize that you have just snapped, or made a tactless comment, or failed to be as supportive as you think you ought to be.

The trouble is, we aren't perfect. And as we have already said, if you live with a migraine sufferer you are part of an eternal triangle, a bizarre ménage-à-trois: you, the sufferer, and the sufferer's migraine. It's not a natural situation, and it is just as stressful as living with any other form of disability.

The difference is that – if you live with someone who is blind, or in a wheelchair – friends are more likely to understand what you are both going through, and that makes things easier. Migraine is such a misunderstood, invisible, often-scorned disability that it is generally overlooked.

Bearing all this in mind, there really is no need to feel guilty when the stress gets to you from time to time. The best way to deal with the situation is to work, with sufferers, to educate people about migraine and refuse to allow people to dismiss it as 'just a headache'. If you show in public that you are proud of your friend's courage and determination, this will encourage other non-sufferers to examine their own attitudes.

Why do you feel helpless?

With any illness, there will always be problems of communication and understanding. Pain is a very subjective experience, and it is impossible – even with the best will in the world – for one person to experience another's suffering or to understand it completely.

To complicate matters, many sufferers find it impossible to express themselves lucidly when they are in the throes of a migraine attack, which makes communication problems significantly worse. If the sufferer cannot tell you how he or she feels, or what he or she needs or wants you to do, it is not surprising that you should end up feeling pretty useless.

Learning to talk to each other about attacks can produce positive strategies which you can put into operation – dispelling the feeling of helplessness.

Practical strategies

Friendship and socializing

Having migraine means that you are never really free of the fear of it. Even if your attacks are infrequent, or if they have been dormant for a while, there is always the vague apprehensive feeling that an attack will come along and ruin your day – right at the moment when you are most enjoying yourself.

As we saw in Chapter 1, this can ruin the quality of life for many sufferers: they may develop an almost morbid fear of making definite plans and arrangements (mellontophobia) and withdraw completely into their shells. It's almost as if they are in suspended animation, holding their breath and waiting for the pain to begin.

You may not realize it, but the chances are that you sometimes make things worse for your friend. How many times have you become impatient at his or her reluctance to make appointments, organize dinner parties, go to parties etc? How well do you disguise that note of impatience in your voice when your friend rings you up at the very last minute and says 'I can't go to the cinema – I've got one of my migraines coming on?'

The trouble is two-fold: first, you have never had an attack so you probably think your friend only has something like an ordinary headache (and headaches often go away when you relax and let your hair down, don't they?), and second, you may feel – consciously or unconsciously – that you are being let down, perhaps even deliberately. Is your friend malingering, just to make life difficult for you? You might not want to admit it, but it's likely you've felt like that sometimes.

It is not just migraine sufferers who face this problem. Susie used to suffer from severe attacks of cluster headache. She recalls:

> At one time, arrangements would have to change at the last minute. Family would 'Tut!' and say 'It's only a headache, for God's sake'. It really made me feel like some sort of freak, as I could assure anyone I would rather be going out for a nice meal somewhere than pacing my bedroom floor and banging my head on the wardrobe doors.

Susie's husband, though sympathetic, felt powerless to do anything to help her:

When my wife was suffering from these severe attacks of cluster headaches which were occurring every day, I had a feeling of complete helplessness. All I could do was offer my sympathy, as I knew she was suffering with terrible pain.

Brian is 57, and has suffered from migraine for many years. He freely admits that his migraine has had a detrimental effect on his social life:

I have lost friends through migraine. When spending a weekend with them, I have had to stay behind and sit in a chair or lie on the bed whilst everyone else went out. Ultimately, they just drifted away.

Dos and don'ts

DO:

- Understand that migraine is not just a headache, that it can be a dreadfully severe form of pain, combined with nausea, uncontrolled vomiting (which may make the headache worse), visual disturbances, shivering or sweating, diarrhoea, pins-and-needles and a whole host of other horrible symptoms. Would *you* really want to go to a party feeling like this?
- Understand that some social activities may induce or aggravate migraine attacks. I'll take myself as an example. Flickering lights make me ill, so I rarely risk going to the cinema. And then there's the weather, too: windy days with bright sunlight are torture for me, as are heavy thundery days and bright car headlights at night. Your friend isn't being awkward or weird – just afraid of being ill yet again.
- Understand that the build-up of excitement over several days can bring on an attack at the most distressing moment – e.g. at a birthday party, or at a concert your friend desperately wanted to go to.
- Make arrangements flexible and say 'Don't worry if you're not well – we can always make another date.' Because you can.

DON'T:

- Grumble and groan when your friend cancels a social engagement or declines an invitation. Sufferers feel ill enough and guilty enough already, without you making them feel worse!

- Exert a lot of psychological pressure to make your friend accept an invitation: that will almost guarantee an attack.
- Accuse your friend of being anti-social or a recluse. Most sufferers would give anything to lead a normal, outgoing social life and go through agonies of guilt and disappointment because they can't. As one sufferer explained to me, 'When you're having an attack, nothing exists except the pain – there isn't room for anything else.' Your impatience and the loss of your friendship would simply add to that pain.

Working with a migraine sufferer

The workmates and bosses of migraine sufferers are often guilty of believing that migraine means unreliability, feebleness and lack of moral fibre. Sometimes they even blackmail the sufferer into believing it too. And yet, many sufferers sustain their career at the expense of the rest of their lives – returning home ill, exhausted and in tears at the end of each day.

The worst thing about migraine and work is the general lack of sympathy which many sufferers encounter. If you work with some-one who has migraine – of if you employ a migraine sufferer – you can help to make life bearable.

DO:
- Stand up for the sufferer, and refuse to let other people belittle his or her illness.
- Show that you understand what the sufferer is going through, and offer practical and emotional support in a discreet and caring way.
- Make sure that a supply of appropriate medication etc is kept at work and that you know how and when it should be administered.
- Ensure that there is a quiet place where the sufferer can rest during an attack.
- Offer to arrange a lift home if the sufferer is too ill to remain at work.
- Talk to the sufferer about migraine; find out all you can; and educate other people in the office to be more sensitive.

DON'T:
- Make the sufferer feel guilty or inadequate, or that giving up and going home is a sign of weakness or unreliability.
- Use migraine as an excuse for a day off work. Challenge others if they do this.

Children

Migraine is very common among children, though it is not always diagnosed as such and does not always follow the adult pattern. Strangely, most childhood sufferers (around 80% in fact) are boys, though the figure is reversed in adulthood, when four out of every five sufferers are female. So the good news for boys is that many will grow out of it – whilst the bad news for girls is that they may 'grow into' it, perhaps during or after the major hormonal changes at puberty.

Migraine – with or without an aura – can be a very frightening experience for a child, and is likely to have an effect upon the child's whole attitude to life, especially if it is not handled sympathetically by parents, friends and teachers.

Margaret suffers from classical migraine, and now suspects that her daughter Kate may also be a migraine sufferer:

> She has many attacks of unexplained stomach pain, followed by headaches, and goes extremely pale. This usually occurs at school, and at first, the teachers would ring me to take her home, but it was happening too frequently. The school doctor suggested it could be migraine. Kate is quite bright and doing well at school, but tries very hard, and the doctor said that is just the sort of child to have them: she puts stress on herself by trying too hard.
>
> We try not to put any stress on her ourselves, and praise her as much as possible, and try to make her relax at home. She hasn't been too bad lately – but, needless to say, her attacks also put stress on me.

There are special paediatric migraine clinics at some hospitals, with trained doctors who can help ease the physical and mental suffering through drugs, dietary therapies and relaxation techniques.

If you are the parent of a child with migraine, statistics suggest that there is a fair chance (60% or more) that you or your spouse, or another close relative, also has migraine – because of the strong hereditary element. It's a good idea for the adult sufferer to share experiences with the child – provided, of course, that the adult is able to transmit a positive attitude towards coping with the migraine!

Make sure that teachers, youth leaders and other parents know about the child's attacks, and brief them in what to do if the child is ill whilst in their care: this will help you reassure the child that there is nothing to fear, for example when away from home for the day.

The other side of the coin is the adult migraine sufferer who lives with a collection of boisterous young children who don't have migraine. Young children find it difficult to understand why Mummy or Daddy is pale and grumpy, and doesn't want to play. The problem is particularly acute for migraine-suffering mothers who have to spend the entire day caring for, coping with and restraining the natural energy of their lively offspring. Many mothers feel guilty because they perceive themselves as 'failing' their children by not being the perfect, ever-cheerful, ever-strong parent.

Another problem is the strong sense of responsibility which mothers naturally feel towards their children. Even under normal circumstances, mothers sometimes feel that they carry a tremendous burden of responsibility: that they alone are charged with ensuring their children's safety and wellbeing. When a severe migraine attack threatens, not only does the parent have to cope with the fear and pain: there are also the children to consider.

Case study Mrs S is a 36-year-old mother of three, and she has suffered from classical migraine for about eight years now. In fact, she had her first attack just after she had given birth to her first little boy.

One of her main worries is the fact that her children are still too young to understand. She says:

I have been lucky in that many of my attacks have happened at night; what I'd do if it happened when the children were running around at full pelt, I really don't know. One sufferer I know has a hyperactive little girl, who's only three.

On the other hand, children can be quite sympathetic, and will often quieten down. What really bothers me is getting back from somewhere I've taken them in the car. To be responsible for getting us all home: that really terrifies me.

It is a good idea to train children from an early age, so that they can learn to be caring and sympathetic when Mummy or Daddy is having an attack. As Jean remarks: 'My children quickly learned to make me honey sandwiches and hot drinks, and memorized where my tablets are kept. Now, they send me to bed and ignore me!'

Some people find it helpful to wear a large sticking-plaster on their foreheads when they are ill, as this helps children to relate to their illness: without it, their migraine is invisible and difficult to comprehend.

Lovers and spouses

Personal relationships can be a real problem for migraine sufferers, because most non-sufferers tend to resent having their own social lives curtailed and restricted by the sufferer's illness. It's not just the fact that arrangements have to be changed at short notice: many sufferers fall prey to mellontophobia – the fear of making any plans at all –because of the ever-present worry that an attack will come along and ruin everything.

Adrienne is 44 and has suffered from migraine since she was a teenager, though since discovering feverfew capsules she has noticed a considerable improvement in her illness. She describes the effects of her migraine on her husband as 'very bad, as my husband is extremely sociable. I worry about going out, which normally brings on a migraine attack.' When she asked her husband to tell her honestly how he felt, he said 'Groan . . . oh no, not again.'

Apart from the social isolation which can result, living with a migraine sufferer is inherently stressful because of all the feelings of guilt, resentment, fear and helplessness which tend to get mixed up with the more positive feelings of love and empathy.

In some ways it is easier to live with someone who has a visible disability, because this at least elicits some recognition and support from family and friends. Migraine, because it is invisible and self-contained, often attracts the unspoken stigma of malingering, hypochondria or 'making a mountain out of a molehill'.

As Mrs M explains, even the happiest of relationships comes under strain when one of the partners suffers frequent, severe migraine attacks:

> As my husband's migraine attacks are so frequent, it is hard to stand by helplessly and watch him suffer so. We have been married for 33 very happy years but we are childless, and only have each other. It is a terrible thing to watch such suffering. We pray that the Good Lord will give the doctors the knowledge one day to be able to help my husband and those people like him who suffer from this terrible affliction.

On the positive side, it is possible for migraine to bring two people closer together, if there is a genuine willingness on both sides to trust, communicate and work together. If you love someone who suffers from migraine, don't add to that person's suffering by making them feel more guilty and inadequate than they already do.

DO:

- Join a support group, and talk to as many other people who live with migraine sufferers as you can. They won't have all the answers, but together you can pool your resources and find support through shared experiences.
- Set up a support group in your area if there isn't one already.
- Talk patiently and with genuine interest to the sufferer. Show that you care and are not implying that he or she is somehow 'to blame'.
- Find out what activities you can enjoy together, and which tend to provoke an attack.
- Encourage your partner to try new experiences by providing a supportive atmosphere. Confidence-boosting will relieve stress and this may in turn reduce the frequency or severity of the attacks. Many migraine-sufferers have a low self-image, often reinforced by their friends and lovers.
- Work hard to develop a good, loving, sexual relationship: some studies have suggested that good, caring sex can relax sufferers and reduce pain.

DON'T:

- Make the sufferer feel you are 'doing him or her a favour' by giving your love and support to an 'inferior' human being.
- Fall into the trap of taking out all your grievances on your partner.
- Try to force your partner to take part in activities which trigger off attacks (e.g. violent exercise).

Helping during an attack

You will be much less of a 'chocolate teapot' if you know what to do and what not to do during your friend or relative's attacks.

Preparations

It's no good waiting until an attack starts and then saying: 'What do you want me to do?'. By then, it's much too late. Your friend will probably find the sheer effort of trying to communicate with you too much to bear, and once again you will be shut out – standing on the sidelines, surplus to requirements once again.

It's a much better idea to make preparations well in advance: to sit down with your friend and talk things over. You will probably find that most sufferers are amazed that anyone should want to discuss their illness with them. Most of us migraine-sufferers are accustomed to indifference and antagonism, but find the idea of a sympathetic desire to know, absolutely novel and intriguing!

At first, your friend may try to shrug the whole thing off – most migraine-sufferers do – for one of two possible reasons:

1. Migraine is a very 'internal' sort of disorder, and sufferers are not generally encouraged to make a fuss about it. In any case, the natural instinct is to crawl off into a corner and hide until you are feeling better.
2. There may be a natural reticence to talk openly about something which causes so much pain – perhaps a fear that talking about the beast may release it from its cage and set off another attack.

Encourage your friend to talk you through a typical attack, and to tell you:

– how it starts: are there any warning signs?
– triggers: are there any trigger factors which you could help to reduce or eliminate (e.g. stress, types of food, noise)?
– things that make it worse
– things that make it better
– medication which your friend takes during an attack.

You may be in a better position to recognize the really early warning signs than the sufferer. Such signs could include mood changes, changes in normal behaviour, cravings for certain foods etc. The best approach is to note any such signs in your diary: over a period of months, you may be able to identify a regular pattern which will help you and your friend to predict and prepare for attacks. You can also make sure that your friend takes his or her medication at the right times, thus reducing the likelihood of a major attack!

If you have done your homework, you will feel a lot less helpless the next time your friend has an attack.

Before it starts

If you have identified a warning sign, draw your friend's attention to it gently.

Next, ensure that any medication is taken early, preferably before any pain starts: once the attack has taken hold, it will be much more difficult to treat.

Make sure that your friend feels you are there to help, but not to get in the way. Take away any responsibilities (e.g. household chores) which may make your friend feel stressed, but don't insist on doing things if your friend wants to carry on being active.

During the attack

The following is a list of some of the things you may like to have handy in case of an attack. You can add to it as necessary:

- Hot and cold gel-filled packs (keep one in the freezer, and the other can be warmed up in a pan of hot water, as needed)
- Hot-water bottles
- Clean towels (to wrap the hot-water bottles, and in case the sufferer is sick)
- Face flannel
- Basin or bucket
- Medication

DO:
- Prepare thoroughly but unobtrusively: no one wants to be continually reminded of attacks by a bewildering array of drugs, hot-water bottles etc.
- Make it clear that you are available and happy to help if needed.
- Relieve your friend of responsibilities: e.g. shopping, telephoning the office, cancelling arrangements, arranging for children to be looked after, cleaning etc.

DON'T:
- Keep pestering your friend during an attack, with questions like 'Are you feeling better yet?'. As one sufferer remarked to me, 'When you are feeling better, you will say so!'. But be around – perhaps in a neighbouring room – in case the sufferer needs something.
- Keep offering food: most sufferers find the very thought of eating absolutely nauseating during an attack. But they may be grateful for a glass of water.
- React with panic or resentment to the onset of an attack: the more calmly you behave, the more calm the sufferer will be and the better able to face the attack and get on with coping with it. Let it become just another event in life, not an inconvenience of disastrous proportions.

General points to consider

It isn't just the migraine-sufferer who needs support and understanding: you do, too. Don't be afraid to ask for it: there is a growing number of support-groups and information resources. If there isn't a group in your area, why not set one up?

Apart from the psychological benefits of talking to other friends and relatives of sufferers, there is always the possibility of arranging valuable practical support – help with childcare, information on new drugs and other treatments (e.g. compiling a list of good alternative practitioners), educating public opinion, quiet places to go if your friend is taken ill in town . . . the options are boundless.

If you need more help and advice, try contacting:
- your GP
- support groups like the British Migraine Association
- libraries (most carry a large selection of books about migraine and related subjects)
- a professional counsellor
- Relate counsellors (who deal with all sorts of questions involving relationships, not just marriage break-ups).

Summing up

- Many of the problems which migraine sufferers face are aggravated by other people's negative attitudes.
- Migraine affects the lives not only of sufferers, but of their families and friends, too: all of these people need help, understanding and support. Don't be afraid to ask for help.
- Trust, sympathy and openness can make life much easier for everyone.
- There are many practical things you can do to help a migraine sufferer, and in doing so you will also feel more valued and useful.

7

Battling On: Self-help
and Hope For the Future

The main point of this book is to help you fight back against your migraine attacks, and this chapter is devoted entirely to the strategies you might consider adopting.

The modern approach to medical treatment is a behavioural one: that is, it encourages the patient not to just sit passively by and wait to be cured by the doctor, but to take responsibility for his/her own wellbeing.

It is the patient's right and duty to take part in the treatment process, and it stands to reason that treatment is going to be more effective if the patient is actively involved and highly motivated. That is why self-help has become so popular over the last few years. Luckily headaches in general, and migraine in particular, lend themselves very well to self-help therapies.

Why self-help?

If you set about helping yourself before and during attacks, you can expect to feel many benefits, including:

- improved morale and hope for the future
- a sense of usefulness (as opposed to that feeling of utter helplessness which so many people lapse into)
- greater physical wellbeing: there are many simple, practical ways of alleviating your own sufferings without coming into conflict with orthodox treatments
- the respect of others (who will see you as a brave fighter, and not just the helpless victim of circumstances)
- the respect of your inner self

Perhaps the greatest argument in favour of self-help is the fact that you have absolutely nothing to lose and everything to gain. Whereas prescription drugs and over-the-counter analgesics are strong substances which can have unpleasant side-effects, self-help therapies use natural methods which will do you no harm and may do you quite a lot of good.

Before you begin

Although the practical tips given in this chapter are in themselves perfectly harmless and are often greatly beneficial to migraine sufferers, they are not intended as a substitute for medical treatment.

If you suffer from headaches, you should first see a doctor, and keep your GP informed of all the strategies you are using. That way, you will keep everyone happy and enable your doctor to formulate a care plan for you which takes account of every aspect of your lifestyle.

Home comforts: physical help at the onset of an attack

Let's say you feel an attack coming on. You've got that awful vague feeling which tells you that pretty soon you're going to be good for nothing, and you start to panic. There's a dull ache on one side of your head, and you're positive it's going to turn into a raging, throbbing inferno. What can you do?

Plenty. There are lots of ways in which you can either stave off a full-blown attack, reduce its severity or simply make yourself feel more comfortable. They are techniques which you can use on yourself, but better still, why not involve a friend or spouse? Your friend will feel needed and involved, and you will be in less pain – so both of you will derive some benefit.

Food and drink

Some people immediately go off the whole idea of eating and drinking, but others find that food and drink can either abort an attack or reduce its effects. Strategies which you might try are:

- a strong cup of coffee – this isn't usually a good idea for migraine sufferers, but if you are a long way from home and have to get yourself back, the caffeine in a cup of coffee can sometimes give you sufficient 'lift' to stave off the attack for a while and get you back to the safety of your bed
- a cooked meal helps some people
- weak sweetened tea and a plain biscuit
- sweet food (one sufferer I talked to swore by honey sandwiches)
- herb tea (try to discover which ones suit you best: camomile is soothing, peppermint excellent for nausea, etc.)
- a couple of glasses of cold water

Acupressure, trigger points and massage

We have already discussed acupuncture as a method of reducing migraine, either by alleviating the pain or by using the ancient Chinese method of redressing the body's energy balance.

Obviously, acupuncture is a complex technique which should *never* be attempted by amateurs, under any circumstances. But acupressure – the art of applying pressure to certain key points of the body – is simple, harmless and can bring considerable relief.

There are several different kinds of nerve fibre in the body. It is thought that this system works by stimulating one type of nerve ending, which in turn blocks the stimulus to the pain nerve endings.

Figure 4 shows the main pressure points on the head, base of the skull, hands and wrists. These correspond to known acupuncture points. With the tip of your index finger (or the knuckle, this is very good too), apply firm pressure to each of the points in turn, using a circular motion. You will probably find it rather painful initially, but try to persevere for at least 15 seconds. You may find it beneficial to apply pressure to two opposing points (e.g. the temples) simultaneously.

The pressure points at the back of the head and neck are common 'trigger points' for tension headaches and migraine: little areas, perhaps the size of a 10 pence piece, of concentrated muscle spasm. It's as if tension builds up in these points, then from time to time extends into the surrounding muscles, causing more generalized pain – a headache.

Trigger points can exist all over the head, neck and shoulders, and they remain 'active' until 'deactivated' by systematic, specialized massage. They are painful to the touch, and you may find that when you press them you feel the pain some distance away: for example, you press a trigger point in your neck but you feel pain in your shoulder.

There are massage therapists who specialize in trigger point therapy, and who will teach you and your friend to work together to eliminate trigger points. Alternatively, you can simply ask your friend to apply firm pressure to each point in turn, and this is quite likely to give you some relief. Each point should be pressed firmly for about a minute. Then a cool-pack should be applied for a few seconds, after which you should stretch the muscles gently to help restore flexibility.

Massage techniques are unlikely to offer a cure for migraine,

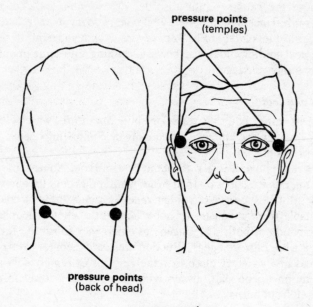

pressure points
(temples)

pressure points
(back of head)

pressure point
(produces deep pain when massaged)

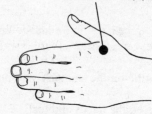

pressure point
(produces tingling sensation when pressed)

Figure 4. Main pressure points

because the causes of the disorder are so complex. Yet even a generalized massage can be very relaxing: and if you are relaxed your attacks are less likely to be very severe. Asking a friend to massage your neck and shoulders can be very soothing, and some people even enjoy a foot massage.

Heat and cold

It seems rather odd that variations in temperature, which can often bring on migraine attacks, can actually be comforting once an attack is in progress.

There are no universal rules about heat and cold. Some sufferers can only tolerate ice-cubes on their head, whilst others opt for a hot- water bottle. But most people can obtain relief by using either hot/ cold packs (available from chemists) or hot-water bottles. Some people use a combination of both. One ingenious emergency substitute for an ice pack is a bag of frozen peas. (But don't refreeze them for eating later.)

Incidentally, never place extremely hot or extremely cold objects directly on to the skin, always wrap them up in a towel to protect yourself from burns.

Here are some suggestions for relief. Try them out, and see which one works best for you:

- hot-water bottle or ice-pack on forehead, temple or nape of neck
- hot-water bottle on stomach (very soothing for abdominal symptoms)
- one hot-water bottle on the stomach, and one in the small of the back
- hot-water bottles on the hands and feet

Some sufferers of mixed or combination headaches find that cold treatments are best for their migraine attacks, whilst warmth works best for tension headaches, but there is no hard and fast rule.

Hydrotherapy

Foot baths

Some people find that the head pain is reduced if they sit with their feet in a bowl of hot water (as hot as you can bear without scalding yourself) for about 15 minutes. This seems to draw the blood away from the congested head area, and may also work by providing a counter-stimulus (heat) to the stimulus of the headache pain.

Enemas

A few alternative therapists suggest warm water enemas as a way of providing relief when constipation is a contributing factor in headache. Enemas can be very dangerous if not carried out by a qualified and experienced practitioner. Perhaps a better way of solving the problem would be simply to go for a brisk walk in the fresh air or take other exercise, and include more fibre in the diet, making sure that you eat regularly.

The inner and outer you

Self-help means looking at your total self and deciding what you can do to improve the way you live your life. All of the following are strategies you could try out, to see if they help to alleviate your migraine attacks:

- Reducing potential causes of stress through planning and self-assertion.
- Becoming generally fitter through regular gentle exercise.
- Learning to relax.
- Eating a sensible and regular diet, free from migraine 'triggers'.
- Managing your lifestyle to eliminate unhealthy aspects, such as smoking.
- Finding remedies (conventional medicine, alternative therapies, herbs etc) which work for you.
- Getting a good night's sleep.

As Dr Anne MacGregor of the City of London Migraine Clinic explains:

Several precipitating factors seem to culminate together to cross the 'threshold' and hence trigger an attack of migraine. It follows that if *any* of these factors can be reduced, it is possible to keep below the threshold and prevent an attack. Factors can be divided into two groups – those you can exert some control over (missing meals, drinking red wine) and those which you cannot (stress at work, travelling). Attacks can be reduced by dealing with the first group. I think patients should be encouraged to be 'fit for life' rather than just treating the migraine.

Coping with stress

There is nothing mysterious or sinister about stress, and there is no way that anyone can ever hope to live an entirely stress-free life. Stress is part of a normal existence, and without it nothing would ever get done!

In fact, stress is very badly misunderstood by most people. It isn't a readily identifiable phenomenon with an independent existence, which acts upon people from the outside. Stress is perhaps best defined as 'coping': whenever your mind and body have to react to and cope with an emotion or a physical event, a certain amount of stress results.

The body's stress reaction is a natural mechanism, designed to help us deal with sudden dangerous situations. Chemicals including the hormone adrenaline are produced, stiffening the muscles and channelling blood into them and away from the body's non-essential organs. Without this reaction, the body would not be ready for 'flight or fight'. Stress becomes dangerous when it is sustained over a long period of time, and the built-up charge (flight or fight) isn't released (e.g. through a game of football, brisk walk etc).

The extent and duration of a person's stress reaction depends not just on the nature of an external event, but on the personality and habitual behaviour of the person undergoing it. Some events, like divorce and moving house, tend to produce a stress reaction in most people; but any event can be stressful. Many headache sufferers live in a state of chronic tension – a self-perpetuating and self-destructive cycle of stress, leading in turn to even more stress and more headaches.

People differ in their ability to cope, but through relaxation, lifestyle management and a whole host of simple strategies each one of us can improve our resistance to stress. And since stress is a major causal factor in migraine and other headaches, this is a point well worth addressing.

Here are a few simple ideas to help you lead a less stress-filled life:

Stress reduction tips

1. *Eliminate caffeine from your diet* Caffeine is a drug present in coffee, tea, chocolate and cola drinks – and several headache remedies. Its stimulant qualities produce physical effects which mirror the body's natural stress reaction – the 'flight or fight' mechanism. Caffeine stiffens the muscles and increases anxiety as well as alertness, making it very difficult to relax. Caffeine can also

reduce the swelling of blood vessels in the short term, but unfortunately, when the drug has worn off, these vessels may swell up to more than their original size, causing 'rebound' headaches.

Cutting down on caffeine – or even better, cutting it out altogether – can have a significant effect on stress levels. Some people experience a rebound effect with their headaches when they give up coffee after being used to several strong cups a day. Rebound headaches can be avoided by cutting down on caffeine gradually, rather than simply giving it up all in one go.

Without relying on the added and unnecessary stimulus of caffeine to help you with stressful situations, you will feel calmer, be better equipped to cope with any stress, and also, importantly, more inclined to look after yourself in other ways (e.g. eating and sleeping well, and taking regular gentle exercise).

2. *Find the right sleep pattern for you* Too much and too little sleep can be precipitating factors in migraine attacks. Anyone who has had an attack after sleeping in late on a Saturday morning knows this, as does anyone who has suffered migraine after a series of late nights.

A small adjustment in the length of your sleep, the times you go to bed and get up, may be all you need to break the cycle of your migraine attacks. Don't forget: if you lie in bed for too long you will delay a meal, and the resulting hypoglycaemia may be enough to trigger an attack. Some people find that simply getting up and having tea and a biscuit is enough to stave off a headache: they can then get back into bed and go to sleep without any adverse effects.

Sleeping pills should always be regarded as a last resort. If you are having difficulty in sleeping, why not try a few of these natural remedies?

- a light bedtime snack and (caffeine-free) low-fat milky drink
- getting up, sitting in a chair and reading until you feel drowsy
- trying hard to stay awake, e.g. by staring at the ceiling
- having a bath
- taking up a sport or going for long walks during the day: the more physically tired you are, the more likely you are to sleep, the better quality your sleep will be – and you may even find you need less sleep!

3. *Get organized* Planning ahead can take a lot of stress out of your life. By avoiding last-minute panics, rushing about, sudden crises and

frayed tempers. You will be doing yourself and your family a great favour. Try some of these strategies:

- each evening, prepare what you will need for the following day
- write yourself reminders (relying on your memory will only lead to slip-ups)
- keep on top of jobs at work and at home: doing a little bit regularly is better than leaving everything to the last minute
- maintain a good store-cupboard, so that if you are too ill or too tired to cook, you know there is always something in the house.

4. *Learn to play the waiting game* If patience is a virtue, it is also a good cure for stress-related headaches. Make a real effort to take a more laid-back approach to daily inconveniences like post-office queues. If may even be worthwhile carrying a book around with you, so that you can turn an annoying wait into a golden opportunity to catch up on your favourite author.

5. *Do one thing at a time* Trying to do more than one thing at once is a recipe for stress. Concentrate on the most important task at any given moment, and refuse to be distracted from it by subsidiary considerations until the job is done.

People may say they can do several things at once efficiently, but the truth is that such virtuosi are thin on the ground. Better to do one thing correctly than to attempt the impossible and have to do both jobs all over again.

If you have an unpleasant but inescapable task to perform, try to get it over with early on in the day: that way, you won't have time to worry about it too much.

6. *Set yourself attainable targets* If you set yourself unreasonable targets, you will constantly fail to achieve them; and this in turn will make you feel a failure. Ask yourself: which are the priority tasks, and which are relatively unimportant? If you set yourself realistic targets, you have the best possible chance of succeeding – and of feeling good about yourself.

7. *Don't be afraid to delegate* However clever and multi-talented you may be, you can't do everything yourself. The really clever and successful people are the ones who can distinguish between the tasks they really must perform themselves, and those they can delegate to

competent subordinates and colleagues. Making use of other people's skills does not mean you are a failure.

At home, get other members of the household to do their fair share of the chores.

8. *Set aside time for yourself* Understand that you are a worthwhile individual, with your own needs and desires. However much you may love your family and friends, they do not own you and in any case, you will be a much more interesting and fulfilled person if you are allowed to do some of the things you want to do.

Set aside 'quality' leisure time for yourself – to be alone if you want to, and to enjoy the things you enjoy doing. Pamper yourself; read a book; have an adventure. And make the most of your weekends: they are times to savour, not just an opportunity to crash out or do the family washing after a stress-filled week at work.

9. *Learn to say no – and mean it* If you know you are over-conscientious and often accept tasks and responsibilities simply because other people are more persuasive, perhaps you need lessons in saying no.

Self-assertion is the art of expressing your opinions, wishes and desires in a positive way which does not threaten other people's opinions, wishes and desires. An assertive person is neither a doormat (passive) nor a steamroller (aggressive): simply an individual who takes account of other people's feelings but in turn expects his or her own to be taken into consideration.

Headaches can make sufferers feel very guilty and inferior, and make it difficult for them to express themselves assertively, especially when they are in the throes of a severe attack. Learning assertiveness makes you feel better about yourself, and reduces the stress which results from being ignored or treated callously by others. This in turn can reduce the frequency and/or severity of attacks.

Assertiveness training courses are on offer all over the country, in adult education institutes and community centres, and an address is also given at the end of this chapter.

10. *Express your feelings* This is an outgrowth of self-assertion. Bottling things up inflicts a great deal of stress upon yourself. It is far better to express your feelings and clear the air.

Talking to a friend can help sort out problems: or, failing that, try writing down your feelings in a diary or on a piece of paper which you can later throw away.

11. *Surround yourself with people and events you can relate to* No one can be happy surrounded by people they don't like or doing boring or over-taxing jobs they detest.

Take a long, hard look at your life and decide if you can reduce your stress by any of the following:

- changing your job
- dissociating yourself from so-called friends who run you down or use you for their own ends
- making new friends and acquaintances you can really relate to
- sorting out family disagreements and tensions
- creating a more interesting and fulfilling social life for yourself

12. *Learn to relate to other people* Migraine is an introverted sort of illness: it tends to cut sufferers off from other people, building barriers between them and making communication difficult, if not impossible.

Some people find that voluntary work or other community-based activities help them to become less inward-looking and better able to relate to other people.

13. *Free yourself from fear* Fear is a terrible, destructive force which eats away at you from within and – unless checked – can grow into an uncontrollable and devastating inner monster.

For migraine sufferers, the fear of being ill can even develop into mellontophobia – the fear of doing anything at all, in case an attack intervenes and ruins everything.

With good medication, a rejuvenated and sensible lifestyle, the fear of an attack should be reduced. Yet we all face daily fears, fears of the unknown; fears of situations which pose a challenge to us.

Through visualization, your fears can be exorcized. By rehearsing the situation many times before it arrives, and rehearsing it in a positive way, you can actually influence the outcome of the event itself. Say it's a job interview: visualize yourself neatly dressed and quietly confident, and answering all the likely questions in turn. When it comes to the day of the interview itself, you will feel as if you have covered all the ground before.

Success breeds success, and a better self-image will follow.

14. *Treat your body with respect* Stress involves both body and mind, and it is vital that you should treat your body well if you are to find relief from the stress which so often leads to migraine.

General fitness tends to improve mental as well as physical well-being, so it is well worth thinking of taking up some form of gentle exercise (not strenuous exercise like squash, as this can actually trigger migraine attacks). It doesn't have to be agony: walking and swimming are excellent, and even stretching exercises can help.

Good breathing techniques – such as those taught in yoga – will help you to find a sense of inner calm, as well as promoting the health of your cardiovascular system (so much a part of the migraine cycle). A simple breathing exercise is given in the section on relaxation.

Last but not least, never skip meals or do without regular breaks. Eating sensibly and at regular intervals helps to prevent the risk of hypoglycaemic migraines, whilst taking even a short break from work at home or the office can be sufficient to break the mounting cycle of inner tension.

Gentle exercise

Exercise doesn't have to be violent or painful: in fact, violent exercise should be avoided, as it can actually bring on an attack. It's always far better to take up some form of exercise which you actually enjoy – such as swimming, or even walking the dog – than to try to stick to something which is a real penance.

Regular exercise tones up the body, stimulates the cardiovascular system and releases natural endorphins which help you to feel happier and generally better about yourself.

Relaxation and migraine

Recent research indicates that sufferers from all types of headache can be helped by relaxation, biofeedback or a combination of both.

Relaxation does not mean just sitting in a chair, reading a book or watching television. You can even be asleep and not be entirely relaxed because your muscles can still be tense.

Real relaxation involves a complete letting go: and you will find that, once you have relaxed all your muscles, it is actually impossible to continue feeling tense or anxious.

Muscle tension, stress and anxiety are all factors contributing to migraine, and if you can learn to relax the chances are that you will not only be able to reduce the frequency of your attacks, but also even alleviate the pain you feel when an attack is in full swing.

Learning to relax

Biofeedback could be described as inducing a state of controlled relaxation. This is achieved by teaching subjects to be aware of the functioning of various parts of their bodies, so that they can in turn discover how to alter that functioning for the better.

There are two main types of biofeedback used in headache:

Temperature control biofeedback is generally used to treat only migraine sufferers. Heat-sensitive monitors are attached to the scalp or the hands. Migraine involves changes in blood flow, and an increase or decrease in blood flow to the hands or scalp shows up on a monitor, as a rise or fall in temperature.

The idea is to learn to raise the temperature of the hands, as this indicates an increase in blood-flow into the fingers and away from the congested areas of the head.

Electrical biofeedback is often used to treat tension headache, though it would be useful for anyone whose headaches involved a degree of muscle tension.

The subject is wired-up to a machine which records electrical activity in the muscles and scalp, and an increase in activity – denoting tension – shows up as a flashing light or noise. The idea is to reduce the sounds or flashing lights by learning to relax the muscles.

Advantages and disadvantages Biofeedback used to be very popular and very trendy, and some doctors looked to it as a sort of cure-all. Since those heady days, the euphoria has given way to guarded approval. Biofeedback certainly can help people to relax and gain control of their bodies, but there are drawbacks:

- it requires machinery, so it can't be practised anywhere
- it isn't easily available (you might have to pay for treatment, or go to a university psychology department; consult your GP first)
- some people can become dependent on the machines, and unable to relax without them.

Relaxation

For most migraine sufferers, simple relaxation techniques are a cheaper, easier and more convenient way of getting to know their bodies. Relaxation can definitely reduce the frequency and severity of attacks, especially in young children; added to which, the feeling of at last being in tune with, and in control of, one's own body can improve self-image by leaps and bounds.

Simple relaxation exercises

The method of relaxation recommended by the British Migraine Association, and the one which is most commonly taught in evening classes etc, is called 'progressive muscle relaxation'. It is easily learned – though it requires perseverance – and can be called upon whenever needed.

Progressive muscle relaxation

1. Lie flat, with a pillow under your head and perhaps another under your knees – your spine should be straight, and you should feel comfortable. Alternatively, you could sit in a comfortable but firm chair. Your feet should be flat on the floor, your back straight and your hands resting in your lap.
2. Close your eyes, and begin to breathe slowly and regularly through your nose. Do this for about 3 or 4 minutes.
3. Imagine that your body is divided into a series of muscle-groups: one for your lower leg, one for your lower arm, one for your neck and so on. Concentrate on the first group, one of your feet, and tense it for a count of 10. Then let go, allowing it to relax completely. The theory behind this is that a muscle relaxes more completely when it has first been tensed. Work your way up your whole body, paying particular attention to the muscles of the shoulders, head and neck.
4. Spend a few moments just lying still, enjoying the feeling of your relaxed body. Then open your eyes, sit up and get on with your day.

There is another form of relaxation – 'autogenic relaxation' – which can help migraine sufferers. This involves repeating verbalized messages to yourself, to help focus your mind on a particular part of your body. It is a blend of relaxation and meditation, and – like meditation and yoga – really needs to be taught to you if you are to obtain maximum benefit from it. To learn more, contact a natural healing centre, or Relaxation for Living.

Audio and video cassettes

Many migraine sufferers find self-help cassettes very helpful, and these can be found in numerous outlets up and down the country – notable health-food shops and bookshops but also (increasingly) in high-street chemists' shops. These may be sold as simple relaxation tapes, as self-hypnosis tapes or as tapes designed specifically to help migraine sufferers. It is worthwhile trying several, as they do vary in quality and don't suit everyone equally.

A charitable organization called Relaxation For Living also produces excellent tapes, which can be ordered by post, and organizes relaxation classes up and down the country. Their address is given at the end of this chapter.

Diet

Eating a healthy diet is a good idea for anyone. If you are in any doubt about what is healthy and what isn't, ask your doctor for some leaflets about nutrition.

If you think that food 'triggers' play a part in your migraine, it is important to try to eliminate them from your diet. However, it is always very advisable to consult your doctor if you are thinking of eliminating any item of food from your diet, just in case you are in danger of impoverishing your diet. Your doctor will help you to draw up a sensible 'elimination' diet if you really need one.

If you are trying to lose weight, you may find that dieting tends to bring on migraine attacks. It may be possible to avoid this if you follow a slow and sensible diet such as the one recommended by Weight Watchers. It's also advisable to avoid sugary foods, as these cause a sudden rise in blood sugar level, followed by a sudden fall – fluctuations which can result in headaches.

Self-assertion

Many migraine sufferers feel guilty about their illness, and may be lacking in assertiveness. The feeling of being at the mercy of one's family or business colleagues can lead to chronic anxiety and depression – which of course won't help your migraine.

Assertiveness courses teach you how to put forward your point of view, firmly but not aggressively, so that you need never again fear being 'steamrollered' by other people.

Travel tips for migraine sufferers

Travel is one of the events which many migraine sufferers find unbearably stressful. Because it is not only a departure from home but also from their normal routine, they fear that the disruption may bring on an attack – and it is certainly true that worries about missing trains, losing tablets and eating the wrong foods can be just as bad as the feared events themselves.

But migraineurs have just as much right to a happy holiday or business trip as any other members of society: and it's all perfectly possible to arrange. It's just a question of planning well in advance: and a minimal amount of fuss beforehand will pay considerable dividends when the day itself comes round.

Here are a few ground-rules for the traveller.

1. *Plan ahead*

Don't leave everything to the last minute. As soon as you know that a trip is in the offing, start the wheels in motion: this means everything from passports, pills and packing to who's going to mind the cat while you're away.

2. *See your doctor*

Go to see your GP and have a chat about your medication needs for the trip. Metoclopramide is useful to take before and during travelling. If it is a long trip, and especially if you are going abroad, you will need to take extra supplies of your drugs, plus a spare prescription if possible (in case of emergencies).

It might also be a good idea to ask for a short letter detailing your illness and the treatment you are taking, together with a list of your drugs along with their chemical composition. This sort of information could be very useful if you have to see a doctor or pharmacist in a foreign country.

It may also be possible to obtain a list of English-speaking doctors in different countries. Such a list is available from the embassy of the country you are visiting.

It's a good idea to learn or write down a few relevant words of the local language so that you can communicate with a doctor, pharmacist or the police in case of emergency.

3. *Check your health insurance*

Don't forget to carry the name and number of your policy with you at all times, and your form E111 if you are travelling within the European Community. You should also have your NHS number and the name and address of a relative who could be contacted if you were taken ill.

4. *Pack your medication safely*

Don't pack your medication in breakable containers, and on no account keep it all in the same bag or suitcase. Just think what would happen if your luggage went astray *en route*!

Divide your medication up into several separate packages and distribute these throughout your luggage, making sure to keep a good supply in your hand-luggage.

5. *Plan ahead for dietary triggers*

When you're on holiday and having fun, it's easy to forget all about your food and drink 'triggers' and over-indulge in *sangria* (made with red wine and oranges) and other local delights.

To avoid mishap, make a list of your triggers and carry it with you: be sure to refer to it before you eat anything 'suspicious', and avoid it if you're still dubious. Better safe than sorry!

Some tour operators and hotels will provide special diets if you contact them in advance. It may be worth enquiring.

6. *Leave yourself plenty of time*

Whatever you do, don't leave all the arrangements to the last minute, or you'll be doing yourself no favours at all. Make sure that all your domestic arrangements are made at the earliest possible opportunity, and leave plenty of time to get to the airport, railway station etc.

This may sound like an awful lot of fuss just for the sake of a single trip, which a non-migraine-sufferer wouldn't think twice about. But isn't it worth it, for the sake of a headache-free holiday?

Unity is strength

One of the worst things about being a migraine sufferer is the terrible sense of isolation, the feeling that 'nobody understands what I'm going through'. Yet there are millions of sufferers just like you and me in this country, and they too feel the need of sympathetic companionship and practical help.

That is why groups like the British Migraine Association and the National Headache Foundation (see end of chapter) have been set up – to bring migraineurs in contact with each other, exchange practical advice and sympathy, and to keep them up to date with all the latest developments in research and drug therapy.

The attack survival guide

Perhaps the single most important thing you can do to help yourself is to learn to accept the existence of your attacks.

This may sound like utter nonsense: how could you possibly deny the existence of a hideous monster who sneaks up behind you every so often and makes your life a misery for hours or even days on end?

Yet isn't it true that there are times – between attacks – when you feel so good, so alive, so normal, that you don't want to even think about migraine. You feel you may never have another attack: the last thing you want to do is prepare for the next one.

Positive thinking is good and necessary. But so is preparation – both mental and practical. The essential point is to strike a balance between denying your attacks and being so overshadowed by them that they reduce your daily life to a constant state of dreadful expectancy – which of course can be self-fulfilling!

Learning to live with your migraine is part of overcoming it. We sufferers need to feel that, even if we are never completely cured, we are strong enough and brave enough to rise above our illness and demand quality and fulfilment in our lives. In order to achieve this, we must first of all develop strategies to cope with our attacks.

Everyone's strategies are different: some people like ice-packs, others like hot-water bottles. There are, however, three good rules to follow:

- take medication early
- take food and drink if you can
- rest

Here are a few more points which may be of help:

1. *Be prepared!*
Like all good Boy Scouts, you should always be prepared. At home or on holiday, keep an 'Attack Bag' somewhere accessible, so that you know you will have all you need to survive an attack with the minimum of discomfort. The last thing you feel like doing in the middle of an attack is crawling round on your hands and knees, looking for the hot-water bottle!

Keep these handy:

- medication
- towel

- bucket or basin
- hot-water bottles, hot/cold packs (keep a cold pack in the freezer at all times)
- any little comforts you find helpful, e.g. fizzy water or dry biscuit (I find a pair of big woolly bedsocks invaluable, as my feet are always freezing during an attack!)
- some people find it helpful to dissolve their medication in lemonade or lucozade
- carry your medication around with you, plus a carton of drink and a small packet of biscuits: you can take these as soon as an attack starts.

2. *Recognize your warning signs and act promptly*

As soon as you know that you are getting an attack, do something about it. Don't – like many sufferers – try to ignore those unmistakeable signs, or you'll end up feeling worse. In order for medication to work, it needs to be taken as soon as possible: don't put your head in the sand, and don't try to be a hero.

If you have an antisickness drug, try to take it before you take a painkiller: it will help your stomach to work better and absorb more of the drug.

Try eating something at the same time as you take your drugs: this will help to raise your blood sugar level.

3. *Obey your instincts*

If you know that you would be better off lying down in a darkened room, try to do exactly that. True, there are times when we are simply too busy to cave in, but treat your migraine with respect, and don't be persuaded into doing anything which you know will make it worse – e.g. a family trip to the cinema. Be firm; be assertive!

If you feel that eating something would make you feel better, then give it a try. If not, don't accept food and drink just to make a loved-one feel helpful!

4. *Relax*

If you have been diligent and practised your relaxation exercises every day for 20 minutes, you should already be feeling some benefit. When an attack comes, don't let yourself be overtaken by panic. Lie down or sit in a comfortable chair, and go through at least a shortened version of the exercises.

5. *Accept help*

Migraine tends to imprison its victims behind a wall of suffering silence; but this is no good at all to you! Being heroically determined is all right up to a point; but if you're too brave and tight-lipped, no one will understand how ill you are. Pretty soon, they will start belittling your illness: 'Well, you look all right to me', or 'You managed all right last time you had an attack' will be the watchwords of your bosses, friends and relatives.

There are times when all of us need a helping hand – particularly when we are away from home, alone or with children, and saddled with the awful responsibility of getting everyone home in one piece.

Don't be afraid to admit that you are ill; and don't be afraid to ask for, and accept, help. It is only by knowing more about us that non-sufferers can come to understand us better.

The British Migraine Association

The British Migraine Association was set up in 1958, by a small group of migraine sufferers who decided that it was time something should be done about migraine.

The Association's aims are to:

- Encourage and support research
- Gather and pass on information about drugs and treatments
- Provide friendly, cheerful reassurance and understanding, with encouragement to fight back by supporting research.

The British Migraine Association now has members all over the world, and is a respected authority often quoted on television and in newspapers. It has some local and national meetings, and sends out a newsletter three times a year. There is a small annual membership fee.

The National Headache Foundation

The National Headache Foundation is an American lay organization set up in 1970, although 800 doctors also belong to it.

The Foundation's declared aims are to:

- Educate the public
- Promote research

- Provide information to sufferers, their families and doctors

Although this is an American organization, there is nothing to stop a British migraine sufferer belonging to it! The annual membership fee is $15, for which you obtain a quarterly newsletter, a diet listing, a book list and a whole host of other very useful little pamphlets and information sheets. The NHA also provides other merchandise – such as relaxation tapes – by post.

Quite apart from these two groups, why not organize a local event in your area to support migraine research and raise awareness of the disorder among non-sufferers? Fund-raising can be fun. If you have creative talents, why not write poems, songs and articles about migraine? Or paint pictures? The more we bring migraine into the public domain, the more difficult it will be for people to ignore it.

Hope for the future

Doctors are working hard to produce a cure for migraine – but this could be some years away. In the meantime, it is up to every individual sufferer to work hard at improving the quality of life.

Migraine is a misfortune, but it is not a disaster. It should not be allowed to assume monstrous proportions and take over your life, squeezing out all the joy and adventure. With the help of professional treatment, and the support of family and friends, you can learn to cope with your migraine and face the future optimistically and with courage.

Summing up

- Self-awareness and self-help are essential factors in successfully combatting your migraine.
- Improving your general physical health and mental well-being will have positive effects on your migraine.
- Changes in your lifestyle may be enough to remove the critical trigger factors which precipitate your attacks. This is much better than taking regular doses of painkillers which may actually give you headaches.
- Planning ahead helps to reduce chronic anxiety and enables you to deal more effectively with attacks if and when they occur.
- Refuse to allow migraine to take over you life.
- Join a support group – or start your own.

Useful Addresses

Chapter 3

NB: You need a doctor's referral letter to obtain an appointment at any of the following clinics.

Hospital neurological departments

The following hospital neurological departments see migraine patients (your GP may know of others):

London: The Elizabeth Garrett Anderson Hospital (women only); The
  National Hospital; King's College Hospital; Hammersmith Hospital
Birmingham: The Birmingham Eye Hospital
Cambridge: Addenbrooke's Hospital
Oxford: John Radcliffe Hospital Paediatric Dept (children only)
Guildford: Royal Surrey County Hospital
Nottingham: Nottingham University Hospital
Newcastle-Upon-Tyne: Newcastle General Hospital
Sunderland: Sunderland General Hospital
Hull: Royal Infirmary
Leeds: St James' Hospital
Preston: Preston Royal Infirmary
Aberdeen: Aberdeen Royal Infirmary
Edinburgh: Western General Hospital
Glasgow: Southern General Hospital
Belfast: City Hospital

Specialist migraine clinics

Princess Margaret Migraine Clinic,
Charing Cross Hospital,
Fulham Palace Road,
London W6 8RF.
A NHS clinic.
This clinic will also treat patients during acute attacks.

The City of London Migraine Clinic,
22 Charterhouse Square,
London EC1M 6DX
A registered charity, relying on patient donations to keep going. Will treat patients during an acute attack, and sees patients between attacks for advice and treatment.

Chapter 4

Acupuncture

British Acupuncture Association and Register Ltd
34 Alderney Street
London
SW1V 4EU
Tel: (071) 834-1012

British Medical Acupuncture Society
67–69 Chancery Lane
London
WC2 1AF

Alexander Technique

The Society of Teachers of the Alexander Technique
10 London House
266 Fulham Road
London SW10 9EL
Provides a list of teachers who have undergone a three-year training.

Chiropractic

The British Chiropractors' Association
5 First Avenue
Chelmsford
CM1 1RX
Tel: (0245) 355-487

Clinical ecology

National Society of Research into Allergy
PO Box 45
Hinkley
Leicester
LE10 1JY
Tel: (0455) 635212
Helps set up self-help groups and produces a pamphlet on exclusion diets.

Action Against Allergy
43 The Downs
London
SW20 8HG

Homeopathy

The British Homeopathic Association
27a Devonshire Street
London W1
Tel: (071) 935-2163

The following offer homeopathic treatment under the NHS:

The Faculty of Homeopathy
The Royal London Homeopathic Hospital
Great Ormond Street
London WC1N 3HR
Tel: (071) 837-3091

The Livingston Clinic
Department of Homeopathic Medicine
1 Myrtle Street
Liverpool
L7 7DE
Tel: (051) 709-5475

Bristol Homeopathic Hospital
Cotham
Bristol BS6
Tel: (0272) 731231

Glasgow Homeopathic Hospital
1000 Great Western Road
Glasgow
G12
Tel: (041) 339-0382

Hypnotherapy

British Society of Medical and Dental Hypnosis
42 Links Road
Ashtead
Surrey
KT21 2HJ
All the members are trained doctors or dentists, as well as being qualified
in hypnosis techniques.

British Hypnotherapy Association
67 Upper Berkeley Street
London W1
Tel: (071) 723-4443

Medical herbalism (phytotherapy)

The National Institute of Medical Herbalists
41 Hatherley Road
Winchester SO22 6RR

School of Herbal Medicine (Phytotherapy)
148 Forest Road
Tunbridge Wells
Kent TN2 5EY
Tel: 0892-30400

Osteopathy

General Council and Register of Osteopaths
21 Suffolk Street
London SW1Y 4HG
Tel: (071) 839-2060

The British School of Osteopathy
1–4 Suffolk Street
London
SW1Y 4HG
Tel: (071) 930-9254
A training school for osteopaths: treats thousands of patients every year, and the fees it charges are much lower than those levied by osteopaths in private practice.

Psychotherapy

British Association of Psychotherapists,
c/o 121 Hendon Lane,
London
N3 3PR
Tel: (081) 346-1747

Relaxation

Relaxation for Living
Dunesk
29 Burwood Park Road
Walton-on-Thames
Surrey KT12 5LH
Tel: (0932) 227826
A registered charity which sets up relaxation groups all over the country. They also produce leaflets and books, and a correspondence course in

relaxation techniques. Or ask at your local technical college, community centre or evening institute.

Chapter 7

Assertiveness

Ask at your local technical college, community centre or evening institute, or contact:

Redwood Women's Training Association
83 Fordwych Road
London
NW2
Tel: (071) 452-9261
Courses for both men and women.

Invergarry,
Kitlings Lane,
Walton-on-the-Hill,
Stafford
ST17 0LE

Counselling

British Association for Counselling
37a Sheep Street
Rugby
CV21 3BX
Tel: (0788) 78328

Self-help groups

British Migraine Association
178a High Street
Byfleet
Weybridge
Surrey
KT14 7ED
Tel: (09323) 52468
(publishes newsletter and helpful leaflets. Supports research projects. Annual subscription £3).

National Headache Foundation
5252 N Western Avenue
Chicago
Illinois 60625
USA
Publishes useful leaflets and a newsletter. Annual subscription $15).

Relaxation

Contact local centres or Relaxation for Living (see address list for Chapter 4)

Further Reading

Anciamo, Damien. *Coping with Headaches*, Chambers, 1987.

Blau, J N Dr. *The Headache and Migraine Book*, Consumer Association, 1990.

Chaitou, Leon. *Headaches and Migraine*, Thorsons, 1986.

Dickson, Anne. *A Woman in Your Own Right*, Quartet, 1982. (Self-assertion)

Hockaday, Judith M. (ed). *Migraine in Childhood*, Butterworths, 1988. (A medical text)

Hunter, Jo *et al*. *The Food Intolerance Diet Book*, Martin Dunitz, 1986.

Johnson, E S. *Feverfew*, Sheldon Press, 1984

Madders, Jane. *Stress and Relaxation*, Martin Dunitz, 1979.

Mansfield, John. *The Migraine Revolution*, Thorsons, 1986. (Contains useful information on clinical ecology.)

Nicol, Rosemary. *Sleep Like a Dream – The Drug Free Way*, Sheldon Press, 1988.

Petty, Dr Richard. *Migraine and Headaches: Treating the Whole Person*, Unwin, 1987.

Clifford Rose, Dr F. and Davies, Dr Paul. *Answers to Migraine*, Optima.

Turin, Dr Alan C and Coleman, Dr Vernon. *No More Headaches! Practical, Effective Methods for Relief*, Robert Hale, 1985.

Wilkinson, Dr Marcia. *Migraine and Headaches*, Martin Dunitz, Optima, 1991.

Index